THE SNIFFER DOG

PATENT STRATEGY BY A STORY TELLER

TARAKRANJAN
GUPTA

INDIA · SINGAPORE · MALAYSIA

Notion Press

No.8, 3rd Cross Street,
CIT Colony, Mylapore,
Chennai, Tamil Nadu – 600004

First Published by Notion Press 2021
Copyright © Tarakranjan Gupta 2021
All Rights Reserved.

ISBN 978-1-63781-430-7

This book has been published with all efforts taken to make the material error-free after the consent of the author. However, the author and the publisher do not assume and hereby disclaim any liability to any party for any loss, damage, or disruption caused by errors or omissions, whether such errors or omissions result from negligence, accident, or any other cause.

While every effort has been made to avoid any mistake or omission, this publication is being sold on the condition and understanding that neither the author nor the publishers or printers would be liable in any manner to any person by reason of any mistake or omission in this publication or for any action taken or omitted to be taken or advice rendered or accepted on the basis of this work. For any defect in printing or binding the publishers will be liable only to replace the defective copy by another copy of this work then available.

Reviews

"Inspired by real-life situations at R & D firms he worked for, Tarakranjan deals with several IP dilemmas technology professional may encounter. Never thought a series of short novels dealing with IP law can put a smile on one's face, but Tarakranjan managed to do so."

– Dr Pim Mul, Principal Innovation Lead at Shell

"*The Sniffer Dog* provides an excellent view of the workings of IP, particularly patents. Tarakranjan's breezy and refreshing style of writing will surely engage many young readers who want to grasp IP concepts quickly."

– Dr Srinivasan Krishnaswami, IP Consultant to Sravathi Advanced Process Technologies Private Limited, Bangalore, India.

"*The Sniffer Dog* is a wonderful exposition of several IP dilemmas technology professionals may encounter. Tarakranjan, who has worked on IP in global R & D firms for years, provides a lucid view on the workings on IP, particularly on Patents. A must-read for young readers who are interested in this very important area."

– Dr Sayam Sengupta, Associate Professor, Chemical Science, IISER, Kolkata, India.

"A patent is an IP right for a new scientific and/ or technical invention. However, the value of the patent will be realized when a patent will be available as a product and/ or service for commercial gain or social impact. In *Sniffer Dog*, Tarakranjan straightforwardly captured all aspects and it is a must-read book for young innovators who wants to make a difference in the world."

– Prof. (Dr) Suprakash Sinha Roy, Manager, Centre for Nanostructures and Advanced Materials, CSIR, South Africa.

"Very anecdotal and refreshing way of addressing the dilemma of every scientist and engineer to protect or not to protect the IP. Narration is like a breeze, very relatable for young innovators at the same time it is very informative."

– Dr Ravi Kumar Meruva, Founder and Chairman, Sensa Core Medical Instrumentation. Hyderabad, India

"Tarakranjan Gupta describes intellectual property issues like you are reading a novel: capturing and worthwhile reading for any other person with some interest in the ins and outs of intellectual property...."

– Bettina de Jong, Chairperson at ISBQPIP, Netherland

Disclaimer

The opinions expressed in the book are those of the author and do not necessarily reflect the official policy or position of the author's current or past employers. The contents of the book should in no way be construed as legal advice and the reader should consult a professional for any consultation. All the characters, organizations and the situations mentioned in the book are fictitious. Any resemblance or similarity to actual events is purely coincidental.

Dedication

Dedicated to loving memory of my mother Mrs Bani Gupta, who's inspiration always remains with me.

Contents

Acknowledgement	*11*
Prologue	*13*
1. Knowing the Feline: The Early Days	23
2. Bell the Cat: The Patent Filing Process in R&D	33
3. Barren Lands: Freedom to Practice	47
4. The Sniffer Dog: Role of IP Analysts	57
5. The Family Felidae: Evaluation of Patent Families	67
6. The Cat Has Nine Lives: Smart Patenting	77
7. Sniffer Dogs on Barren Land: The Importance of Provisional Application	85
8. Alone in the Battlefield: The Story of An Individual Inventor	93
9. Tail That Wags the Dog: The Claim Language	103
10. Set the Cat Free: When Not to File a Patent	111
11. All Cats are Grey in the Dark: Dilemma of Researcher	125
Appendix	133

Acknowledgement

My special thanks to Pousali Gupta for her constant endurance during my writing habits in odd hours and encouraging me as always. My respect to my mentors—Dr. Srinivasan and Dr. Pim—who have been only speaking highly of me. Thanks to my colleagues and project-students whom I met across at different phases of my career—Anurag, Mehak, Bibha, Aishwariya, Lipi, Lateef, Prerna and Shivani—those who directly or indirectly helped me to shape up my understanding in IP for different situations. Thanks to Surendra, my ex-colleague, who has also motivated me to complete my manuscript on time.

Prologue

Building the Second Island

"I want to be a bus conductor," I replied to my arts teacher in primary school. The entire class was laughing in different tunes. I was responding to a common question asked by my teacher and she was taking answer from us one by one.

The teacher was amused "And why so?"

I responded with confidence, "The bus conductor always holds money in his hand. I have seen a lot of currencies inside his bag too. So, he must be a rich person?" The teacher could not ask anymore question thereafter.

Since childhood, many of us have some career ambitions and the choice of some specific options. The road maps may not be clear even during college or university days but we had something in mind as our *future goals*. However, I didn't have much thought about that. I used to live in the "present." When I did complete my PhD and post-doctoral research, I assumed that the research and development path would be my career choice. Actually, there was no scope for a choice. Rather, I had to grab at any opportunity that was available at that time. My entry to the intellectual property (IP) professional world happened just like that. Returning from France in early 2005, I was desperate to find a job to support my family. Later on, I experienced and slowly understood that I had two passions co-existing inside of me at the same time. The first one was that of the technologist and second one was that of the IP professional. The problem was that I could play only one of the roles at a time between these, since they were complete opposites. With time, I realized that I cannot leave one for the other. Thereafter came the year 2008 which showed us the economic and job uncertainty. That was the time I realized that I may need to build additional skill sets to remain afloat in the career hunt. I do not mean that it was important to be the *jack of many trades*, but building a "second island" was absolute necessary. One passion— the first island—would drive my job and the second would fulfill my other dream.

Lunch with Srini

A few years ago, I was having lunch with my early-days' mentor, Srini, at an almost vacant restaurant at Marathahalli, Bangalore. During the casual discussion he asked me how I perceive the role of an intellectual property analyst.

I replied to him, "It's like a sniffer dog."

He was amused, "And why so?"

I replied, "Because an IP analyst searches for hidden references and analyzes them to secure the IP for an individual or for an organization. If the IP is compared with a vast battle field, a sniffer dog is responsible to find the hidden mines and de-risk the movement of soldiers by showing them safe passages."

Srini thought for a while and said, "If you are planning to write a book, it's not a bad idea because a sniffer dog has a number of experiences to share." I did not think of writing a book at that time. Actually, I neither had a wish to write a book nor had I the time. If at all I needed to write a book, I would leave it for my old age in the form of an autobiography, provided I get some "success" in my career. I had no idea what success in one's career could stand for and whether the journey would determine the success or the destination?

I was happily sailing through my life as a program lead in water technology in a global company. In 2016 December, out of the blue, the organization announced that Water R&D would no longer be continued at Bangalore and I was asked to find a job. I had six more months to find an alternative. I could not think of how I could be released in the middle of nowhere after providing my service diligently for over a decade! I thought it was a scar in my career, it was an injustice! I had no idea how I would spend next six months—whether I would continue to do a good job and prove myself to management or build something else outside looking forward. I had two options for next six months. Either to find a job or to build a start up believing on my ability. I accepted the reality that life will not be same as before.

There were a few things I started to practice since then:

1. Remaining prepared—we do not know what is coming next, be it for better or for worse.
2. Accepting new realities or situations. That is the first step of success.
3. Always looking forward to opportunities to the alternatives and doing better.
4. Remaining optimistic in hard times.

For the first time, I realized my "career" as an independent establishment outside any organization I have worked for. Somehow, I had to build a second island for me.

The second island

A poor fisherman sailed to the deep sea in search of fish. The day was not going well for him, as during his return, a sudden storm built up. The boat capsized and the fisherman was fighting in waves for his life. Over time, he lost the hope and was about to surrender his life. When he was about to lose his consciousness, a boat arrived with a few people who pulled him in and started the journey to the opposite side of the coast. Slowly, their boat was moving towards the deep sea. The fisherman was very surprised. He had no idea how many hours passed by, but the boated ultimately reached a beautiful island. The fisherman had more surprises in store for him. Unknown men and women came rushing in, put him on a chariot,

Prologue

offered flowers and escorted him to a king's palace. They eventually decorated him with royal dress and offered to seat him on the throne. The fisherman was so surprised and thought this must be a hallucination or that, post-death, he had reached a supernatural world. After the initial brain-fogging was over, he realized that all the people around him perceived him as their king.

He turned to his nearest standing office bearer and asked him, "What is happening around here?" The guard said, "Sir, every year in the rainy season, we search in the sea for a new king. After a prolonged search in a stormy weather, we found you struggling in water for life. We brought you to our island and made you our king for a year. This is our rule since the ancient times."

The fisherman was very surprised now. After thinking for a while, he asked again, "So I am your king for a year only. What would be my fate when the year comes to a close?"

The reply was more polite, "Sir, we will carry you to another island that is a bit far from here, but that is an abundant one. No one could live there. The island has a forest. The beasts eat the people we leave. If not, the person dies of starvation for sure."

The fisherman who was crowned king now felt afraid. Days passed by. The new king enjoyed his monarchy, but began to lose sleep thinking of his year-end fate.

One day, he asked his prime minister, "If I am the king, would you obey my any direction?"

The prime minister replied, "Yes sir, but you cannot change your faith at the end of the year. It's in our rule book."

The new king said, "No, I would not ask for that. I would like a few of the workers to go to that distant and abandoned island to cut the forest and start the agriculture."

The prime minister obeyed new king's directions and arranged the workforce accordingly. After a few months, the new king asked the minister to send few more families to start building homes and some small-scale industries on that island. This time too, the minister followed the directions. The year-end approached and it was time for the king to bid goodbye to all of the island's inhabitants. They changed his dress for his old clothes, took off the head gear and a few people accompanied him in a boat which started its journey towards the other island. However, as the boat reached that island the companions in boat were really surprised. It was no more an abandoned island with a dense forest! The farmers, workers and inhabitants were running towards the boat to see their "king." They welcomed him to the island which was completely transformed into a fertile land with people living. The fisherman didn't lose the "monarchy." He turned an abandoned, hostile island into a habitable, prosperous kingdom. There, no one could terminate him. He happily started to rule his island thereafter.

Our choice of the second career in parallel is like this "second island." It's not only important to build a second island to deal with economic uncertainty, but also to live with the passion. The career is not only about sticking to a job and performing diligently, it's about building a room for passion and opening a second world to discover oneself.

Apart from a personal goal, an intellectual property (IP) professional should have more than one option to deal with a problem many a times. The plan B should be ready always. It's a part of IP de-risking strategy.

Retrospect of a Sniffer Dog

In the corporate world, some people stay in same organization over the years, while others change jobs frequently. I had not much clue at the beginning of my career about why people leave their jobs. Somewhere, I read that people leave because of the manager. Later I realized that my assumption was only partially correct. With my experience in the corporate world, I realized the "efferent" and "ambitious" people leave their jobs to learn and develop new skill sets, particularly in first few years. Later, the same people change jobs in order to exercise the different skill sets they have acquired over the time. In reality, no organization could use more than thirty percent of one's skill set. Rather than anything else, the business framework would not allow much choice. However, an efficient employee with a versatile skill set would not be satisfied at the organization where only a part of his skills is being utilized. If he/she stays much longer than the "required" time, he/she can lose the sharpness acquired in other skills in the past. So, the best way (or probably the only way) to mitigate the risk is to find another job where some other portions of his/her abilities can be utilized. However, after sometime the same phenomenon would prevail there too. So, it would trigger another job change! However, is there any other way to get a career satisfaction? Mind, it is not about the job satisfaction of course. The job is merely an enabler to career growth but we often mistake a job as a career. If you refer to the story of the second island, that is the answer to a satisfying career. Entrepreneurship, writing, teaching and training in a parallel job are some good starting points. This would not lead to job security. Rather, it would secure career aspiration. Job security in itself does not exist as no job is ever secure. What we could do is to secure our career? In the next few chapters, I have demonstrated a few model situations for learning and growth in different organizations over different time periods in Intellectual property. Perhaps those experiences were my raw materials to build my second island?

A journey named pHNiNE

"Only a handful of start-up companies get some success, are able to withstand against all odds and ultimately sustain themselves. It's not easy!" Dr Singh put me on alert. We were discussing over coffee on an evening in Bangalore. This person earned my respect over time and,

Prologue

to me, he had far more knowledge than a process engineer. He had many points of views on business, marketing, technology, planning and execution. So, rather than a cautionary note, I memorized his words as advice!

When I thought of building a second island, I listened to my heart over my brain. Could I initiate an organization that could cater to the IP needs of individuals and organizations? There are thousands IP firms in India. What would be the differentiator? What would be the target customer base? Before thinking about the goal, operations, target market, what I had decided with was the name of the company: pHNiNE. The background was the constant struggle and challenge at the Water R&D laboratory over the years with all my team members to keep the pH of the solution at 9 in order to optimize a redox reaction.

After a year, I came out of pHNiNE Private Limited, leaving it to safe hands to join as a Water Technologist again in another global water treatment company. I felt that at least the initiation was a success for my second island. I will love to see it grow with time.

CHAPTER ONE

Knowing the feline: The early days

A little more than fifteen years ago, I landed at Bangalore airport by Jet Airways to attend an interview at a multi-national company. By that time, I had completed my post-doctoral research tenure in France and returned to India to look for a job in a research and development organization. The interview I was due to attend was not for an R&D position. The position title was IP analyst. My first one-on-one interview at the Bangalore campus was with Swamy Krishnamoorthy, who was leading IP group. After my formal introduction, he asked me, "Do you know what is IP?"

I didn't spend much time thinking and replied, "IP means Inter-penetrating Polymer." As a polymer and membrane researcher in IIT Kharagpur, I came across this term quite often as this was one of the prime areas for development. Even while sitting in the early morning flight to Bangalore, I was thinking, "Wow! This company has a separate division for Inter-penetrating polymer. I have only seen this as a subchapter in the polymer materials book that I used to consult." So, Swamy was disappointed.

I had no idea what he was thinking before he uttered his next question, "Do you know about the patent?"

I responded with a nod, "Yes, I've heard of it." Swami was satisfied that at least this guy had heard about something called a "Patent".

So, he asked the next question, "Have you seen a patent document and what it looks like?" Now this was beyond my knowledge. A series of interviews followed thereafter and at the end of the day I found myself exhausted, dejected, sitting at the airport and waiting for my return flight to Kolkata. My perception was that a patent is a difficult thing and research and development needs to worry about it, if someone wants to file a patent and wishes to practice the "new thing." However, almost one month after that eventful day I got a phone call from HR who informed me that I had been selected for the job. Still, till date, I do not have any clue about what triggered my selection or what Swami and the others found in me and realized that I would be the "right" person or "right" fit!

Knowing about the Felines

On May 16, 2005 morning I reported to my job. Swami welcomed me and introduced me to other team members. They were not less than twenty at that time, I guess. After I got some time to sit at my desk with my stationery and files and had settled a bit with the new feeling of my first job environment, Swami came back. He told me that as I was new in IP and needed to be coached, he selected a senior person in his team to guide me during the early days. I was following him from the first floor of the Venus building to the ground floor of Uranus. I thought I would definitely struggle to get back to my desk as I realized that all the nooks and corners of each floor were the same, with identical numerous desks and partitions.

Srinivasan was in his late fifties. Swami introduced me to him. I recalled that he would have attended my technical presentation session and perhaps he interviewed me too one-on-one during that interview day. Swami left shortly after, handing me over to Srini. Srini asked me to pull a chair. The first question he asked me was, "When and why should a person file a patent? What "rights" does he get if he gets a patent?" He purposefully did not mention the word "granted with a patent" as my understanding was limited at that time.

I replied, "If a person gets a patent, he can practice his invention." Srini did not say that I was wrong directly to me. Rather, he started to explain and I went into listening mode.

"The process of getting a patent is like *belling a cat* and that's it. If you bell the cat, no one else can bell the same cat anymore. No one can bring the cat home now. However, nowhere is it mentioned in law whether you can or cannot bring it to your home."

I tried to put in an argument, "If I belled the cat, then cat is mine and I can bring it home, isn't it?"

Srini calmly replied, "No, not at all! The patenting process is like blocking others from practice. Whether you can practice or not, it's a different ball game and the exercise is called the '*freedom to practice search and analysis*', which you will learn later."

It was the most important lesson for me on that day that patenting means "blocking." It was difficult to digest for a fresh joinee who came from an academic research background. During the next three years in that organization, I learnt the cat and mouse game of the patent and the role of an IP analyst as one of the very important stake holders.

Before I left Srini's desk for lunch, I asked the most important question of my career, "What is meant by an IP analyst?"

Srini smiled and replied, "IP means Intellectual Property and you are the analyst."

In next few years, I realized the bigger roles of IP analysis. It is almost like the trained "Sniffer Dog" in a bomb squad or military operation to search for the possible danger to de-risk the operations. Since 2005, I came across five companies, faced and dealt with different IP-related situations. On every occasion, I learnt from my mistakes, from my mentors and from my office buddies. I started my Ph.D in IIT Kharagpur on membrane separation of water. The *Water* did not leave me and IP could not let me down. I am fortunate to continue a career balancing my learning in technology and IP at the same time. It was difficult at the beginning but it is a new experience to see both sides of the coin. Scientists and inventors are passionate and protective of their innovation; while an

IP analyst's work is to challenge the invention, shaping or reshaping the idea, helping them to design around and secure the practice the right way. Understanding each other is the most important behavioral tool in the journey.

The Warriors

While joining of my first job at Bangalore, I came to know about two important things. Apart of IP analysts in Swami's group, he also had a few IP agents. The agents used to write the patents and translate the invention into a "legal" document. I did not have much clue, but what was important to me was that I was supposed to work with a patent agent in my group—someone named "Seema," who was also a PhD in Polymers from IIT Bombay and she was on maternity leave at that time. Later on, while working together on different IP projects, I understood the importance of the Patent/IP agent. Writing the patent is an art. The patent agent or drafter is rather a patent scientist who knows the technical subject matter very well on the one hand, and the patent acts and rules on the other. If a sniffer dog could identify a safer place to plant a mine, the patent agent could safely and strategically plant a mine of appropriate quality. Even an agent can design a mine that would not be easily traced by the radar or detectors. I had seen several patent applications drafted by Seema. At the beginning, it felt difficulty to understand the patent language. Why did she choose the most difficult language to explain a straightforward innovation? Why was she repeating the same thing over and over again in the patent application text? The most important part of the patent is "claim." It is found at the end of the patent document. The "claim" is the invention. What she used to do was to make a ring fence around the invention by appropriate legal language. Another objective was to hide the invention from the radar of online patent search engines or databases available. She was very good at "anticipation." When she used to mention that she thought that a specific part of the invention would have been already covered earlier, I got an alert. Many a times, she proved herself to be right. Many a times, I unearthed many references and inventors who had no idea about their existence. Seema included those references during her drafting to represent very good quality applications. Working together in a team is the open secret to becoming successful in IP. In IP, we receive less teaching and guidance from the books and more from the hands-on experiences. Seema and I worked together for almost three years before I accepted my next opportunity as a patent landscape and competitive analyst in another multinational company.

And the Canines...

The scope of work and learning for an IP analyst vary from one organization to another. The learning patterns and rhythms also change as we go up the career ladder. In my first company, I had to learn patentability, freedom to practice, as well as patent landscaping in a short span of time. I learnt a lot from my mentors and peers in parallel to regular training sessions . My second organization decided that patentability, freedom to practice, infringement and invalidations are fully "legal activities" and only should be operated or handled by the attorneys. So, my role was limited to patent landscaping and competitive analysis. In next few chapters, you will see a bunch of short stories or situations I had encountered at different levels of my maturity. It is not about how successfully I had dealt the situations. In some occasions, I think I was right. Sometime, I believe I could have done it in a better way. The most important thing was learning because, in IP analysis, no two situations are identical. So, no book can teach or refer you on how to address the need.

When a sniffer dog enters a battlefield, it does not know who planted the mines, where they were kept, in which pattern the mines were planted or distributed over a field. Rather, it has to carry out its job completely depending upon its previous learning, getting some help from "intuition" and "anticipation." Sometimes, a sniffer dog's olfactory system provides wrong signals and it is not able to track the mines properly. It's a part of the game. A good sniffer dog is one that makes a mistake, learns and corrects itself. Learning from lessons from one battlefield to another, the sniffer dog becomes more clever, more cautious and more alert. It can correlate the things, join the dots, everything happens in the canine brain. The outcome becomes better and better by the days.

CHAPTER TWO

Bell the Cat: The Patent Filing Process in R&D

A disappointment

"I do not mind much that I have lost the opportunity to file the patent, but it is terrible to accept that my five years of working went in vain and carries no meaning." Riaz seemed to be broken down. He was looking shattered sitting in a break-out room. Only yesterday he had returned from the west coast US refinery. He looked exhausted due to the jet lag, but more because of the disheartening news he had received on his arrival at office. The news was really terrible! My fellow IP analyst Suresh had found an earlier patent reference and, on the basis of this, the whole project carried out by Riaz turned out to be neither a novel nor a patentable subject matter. We came to know about this only when the management decided to file the patent application and Suresh got involved in a patentability search. I did not know what to tell to Riaz. It was a hopeless situation.

Almost everybody with a technical background in the R&D industry knows that patenting is the most convincing way to protect the invention. It ensures the safe commercialization of the invented process, product or article. However, the start-up organizations with innovation as a driver often face difficulty in step-wise planning for patenting the invention. Sometimes, big industries lack in planning and end up with losing a granted patent like the incident mentioned above. The inventions are continuously associated with the R&D organization. Mainly two questions are floated around—how to approach and when to approach professionals for patenting. One of my ex-colleagues from a multinational had a brilliant idea incepted earlier in his project dealing with the effluent treatment. He had his initial experimental data set ready in 2013. The management wanted him to dig a bit more, asked him to refine the innovation to make it a sharper one. The process was allowed for a pilot trail in US. He achieved a fantastic experimental outcome of the process at demonstration scale. Thereafter, the management decided to file a patent application. At that moment, in early 2017, the IP analyst did a patentability search and informed that there was a close shave with one PCT application filed by a Canadian company. Ultimately, he was left with two immediate choices. Either to design around his innovation or to abandon the idea of filing. A distant third choice would have been to approach the Canadian company for cross-licensing, if their patent was already granted in US and Europe as designated states. Anyway, it was an additional burden of time, frustration and disappointment. No choice was probably left to get the innovation protected in its original form.

This haunts me with the second question I raised in the earlier paragraph—when would be the right time to put the nail? I have deliberately put ahead the example related to the "second" question as that is what provoked me to pen down this book. Nevertheless, the bigger question rises at that moment, does the patent need to be filed at all? Rather, does one need to bell the cat or not?

To be or not to be

Even before the question—"What is the right time to file a patent?"—is asked, the decision should be made on whether it is important to file a patent at all. Even though it is ensured that the invention qualifies for the conditions of patentability. The term "decision to patent filing" is often decided by the technology and business strategy of R&D organizations. If the strategy is to "quickly" publish the invention to ensure the freedom to practice, there is very little room for thinking. The idea is not to bell the cat at all. The decision is to push it to the open street so that no one else can bell the cat. In many cases, organizations make this option if the "subject of invention" is not related to or linked to business profit and hence, it does not qualify to earn "protection." However, two different scenarios could appear in this case. If the organization and the business wish to ensure the "freedom to practice," then it needs to get published in a journal or be made public as soon as possible. There is always a risk factor that a competitor can sneak in with a patent application if the publication process gets delayed which puts a bucketful of water over the strategy. However, if the business makes an estimation that the invention has no "earning power," they could simply follow a happy-go-lucky mode. Clearly, in my friend's case, as explained above, the business could not estimate the potential of "patenting" within a reasonable time. They delayed in deciding on patent filing which left the innovation caught in the middle of a crease like a hesitant runner in cricket. Some organizations have a more aggressive patenting strategy so that they go for every invention to file. The advantage is that it eradicates the dilemma.

When the cat is not allowed to come out of the bag

I was almost drenched as it was raining heavily at Bangalore and there was some distance to cover by walking between the open parking are for the visitors and the block A of the apartment complex. Akbar was waiting at his door and I found him holding a towel for me. I said, "If you would have gone down with an umbrella, it would have been better." Akbar was quick in reply, "Last time I went with an umbrella to visit a shop nearby during a heavy down pour. While returning, my next neighbor found me at the main entrance and requested me to borrow the umbrella so that he can go out for two minutes. It never returned to me. I asked him, "You could remind your neighbor to return that." Akbar was bemused, "He had three umbrellas of same color and same maker, I could not identify mine. After that incident, I have put my name on the new umbrella with a permanent marker." We both were laughing a bit as I entered into his well-furnished drawing room.

After initial gossip was over and her wife Mahua brought the fruit juices in decorated glasses on a tray, we changed the topic of the discussion. I asked Akbar, "How is your office, anything new in R & D?" Akbar was looking at my already half-filled glass rather than interested to have a sip from his own that was still left on the tray. He anticipated the lines between my words. He started in a relaxed voice, "Whatever the new things I bring on the table, my manager is not ready for filing patents. It's contrary to my earlier manager, who insisted, every new idea was needed to be filed whether it was important to business or not." I was interested to know the reason. "So, you guys are publishing everything in journal or open literature?" Akbar replied "No, he thinks that we would keep those secret to ourselves."

I understand his mind set. A scientist who is working in a multinational feels a satisfaction when he applies for a patent. When it is granted, the satisfaction turns into a "success". Even a journal publication will add a feather to his hat. However, what he explained was a stagnant situation.

The situation is different from the earlier section, where the business does not want to file a patent, but it is ready to publish the reports to ensure the *practice right*. Here, the business just wants to sit idle with no intention for publication in any form. Akbar mentioned the logic. His manager thinks, if the invention (if at all) gets published in form of patent application, then someone interested or a competitor can make a little modification and start practicing. In our IP language it is called *designing around*. In some technical areas it's not difficult at all. The situation is like you have belled a cat, your competitor sees the cat, studies it well and comes back with a "similar" cat that will do same job of mouse hunting (bringing new business). A designing around is not always done for applying for a fresh patent. Some time it's carried out just to avoid the scope of an already granted patent or patent-to-be granted. Designing around is a tool to get a business by circumventing the legal implications.

If the inventor publishes the invention in form of report or journal only, then the competitor even does not even bother to do a design around. The competitor could just copy the invention and start practicing! So, in both the cases inventor is the loser. An important business policy in R & D is to keep some of IP in form of "Industrial secret".

The risk is that if a competitor invents (or re-invent?) the exactly same thing and applies for a patent that blocks the original inventor from practicing. In some cases, the "secrecy" may be lost somehow from the R & D group, even though the employees are bound by the agreement and are not supposed to share the "confidential" information with an outsider.

The time to bell the cat

Let's settle with the fact that the organization has decided to file the patent and has found its importance. The new idea has been developed and the indications of workability have been captured but it's lacking substantial data to support it. Then, the patentable subject matter can be filed as a "provisional application." The rule is to file a complete application within one year with a complete specification, that is, with all supporting data and evidences. The fee for the provisional application is less than a normal (non-provisional, full specification) application and it gives you the timeline of a year to further work on the invention. The date of the invention (priority date) stays as the filing date of the provisional application. If anyone comes up with the same invention after the date of provisional application, the original application stays as "first to invent." The idea is to bell the cat early, so you need a harness. It is not really necessary to wait for a bell. What else can be done if you do not find a justification to file a non-provisional within a year or failed to collect sufficient "evidence?" Simply drop the idea. The provisional application never gets published. No one other than the patent office would know about this filing. If you find a suitable reason to work on the subject matter later on, you can even wait more than a year to start working on the invention, design around if necessary and make it more robust. You would only lose the *priority date* (date of invention) and pray that another cat did not sneak in between!

Get ready for the cat and mouse game

Even before thinking to file a patent application, you need to ensure that no one has belled the cat already.

If you approach a patent attorney with an "invention," they could draft that in a legally acceptable patent format and file your patent application at an appropriate patent office. However, it's your obligation to ensure whether the process, product or article you wish to protect has been *invented* by you at all. I am not using the most cliché phrase "re-inventing the wheel" because "re-invention" does not exist. So, if your process, product or article was known in the public domain before you put forward the patent application there is a higher possibility that the patent application will be rejected during the prosecution, which is called "office action" in patent language. The situation is like you are trying to fish a cat which was already belled by someone. In patenting language, it's called a "prior art". Here comes the role of an intellectual property analyst who knows patent laws on the one hand, and technology on the other. They could "define" the invention. Please remember, if you cannot frame your invention in one sentence it's not an invention at all. Rather, it means that you are not sure and the matter needs further modification, correction or rectification. So, if you could explain your one-line invention, then IP analyst would search for "patentability," which is the term associated to find the same or similar process or product or article which already exists in public domain.

After the "patentability search," he or she would come up with one of the three possible suggestions. The first one is—if there is no prior art and the "invention" is patentable, go for it. He or she would work with a patent attorney and a patent drafting team to construe the invention. Second, if the "bull's eye" type of prior art is found, he or she may suggest dropping the idea for patenting because, the patent office would definitely find the same reference during the patent examination process and it would ultimately lead to the loss of time and money. If the cat has been belled by someone else, find some other cat. The third, if he/she finds a very close prior art and thinks that it's still possible to get through with a patent with a minor modification of the invention; he/she can still suggest a "design around" it. A patent analyst mainly uses the search tools to search in the journal and some patent literatures to find the prior arts. This way, you can pro-actively minimize the risk of patent application rejections based on an existing prior art.

Summary of the game

One of the major aspects during the entire discussion on the patent filing is that I did not explain the role of the IP analyst in the early stage of the patenting process. Does the involvement or role of an IP analyst start just before the patent application filing or even before? Does a "sniffer dog" have a bigger role to play other than finding a planted bombshell in the landscape or guiding a road diversion (design around)? Remember the story of my friend mentioned at the beginning. The sniffer dog was brought to the mine field. He rightly identified the danger. However, it is never too late for him to guide and modify the situation (invention) to an alternate route.

De-risking the process

The smart way to ultimately obtain a granted patent starts with the de-risking the process of filing. One needs to define the cat; move the cat to a corner to catch it and bell it. If the pre-assessment found that anyone else has already belled it, then there is a need to redefine the process and go for another cat. When we need to bell a cat, we need to bell it correctly so that the cat remains belled. If we wish to bell the cat without planning, assessing and de-risking, the whole process would yield nothing.

The ideal patenting process we have discussed so far contain these steps:

Defining the invention (or idea).

Involving an IP analyst at an early stage to search for the "novelty" of the possible invention.

Being aware of prior arts and going for a design-around early if required.

Filing a provisional application if the sufficient supporting data/justifications are not ready.

Utilizing the one-year window for working on the invention.

Preparation of a non-provisional application with draft claims.

Allowing a "patentability" search by IP analysts on draft claims to assure that the claims are "patentable."

In case the IP analyst finds "prior art," he/she needs to design around the claims/invention.

If the data and examples are ready, the complete patent specification can be filed (non-provisional).

CHAPTER THREE

Barren Lands: Freedom to Practice

Gilbert syndrome

"We would rather go for a quick publication for this…" he talked, looking straight into my eyes while fiddling with his pen between index and thumb. Dr Simon Gilbert sounded so sure that it would serve the purpose. As a water treatment technology head, he had a strong influence on our Bangalore R&D team. A quick publication meant publishing an article on our new water treatment process in an international journal. After a pause, he added, "Our technology maturation plan does not prefer a patent application. Since this is not our core business area and we are not selling the technology—rather, we are only developing this to implement at our site—we don't care if someone copies this. We only need to ensure that no one could file a patent on this and we have a "practice" right. A quick publication would ensure that." He did not expect any feedback from my side. I knew from my previous experiences that I could not win any argument there. The person was a very good technologist, excellent in process development and he thought that he could manage the IP challenges associated. Even I was confused at that point. Perhaps he was right. Perhaps there was no risk and perhaps I was worrying too much. We were not doing any "business" with this invention. Why should I think of protecting this with a patent application? Why do we need unnecessary extra funding for a patent filing, attorney fee, annual fee and so on? A cloud containing confusing and self-contradicting statements engulfed my thought process. I left his desk leaving the action items for him. However, it left me with a chronic unease in my grey matters. I did not know why I was not completely satisfied with his arguments. The time passed by...

When the cat came out of the bag...

It was a gloomy afternoon. I received a phone call from an IP analyst from our office building while sauntering in our wet lab. As of then, it seemed like nothing in his voice could disturb me, "I have found a company offering site-trials of similar technology in Europe. I have shared the website with you, kindly check your mail inbox." Sriram was a person with minimum words. So, I did not show enthusiasm for any further discussion with him. After a coffee break, I opened my laptop and double clicked the link he shared with me. I was interested in the Biotech company which had a steady business growth since 2008. I was amazed at how a company with a knowledge base in biotechnology could jump into water treatment. Anyway, nothing wrong in the bio-treatment of water for oxidation, purification and all to try at. I went a step ahead and searched in their patent publications. One of the recent PCT publications in 2016 drew my attention. Although it was an electrochemistry-based solution for water treatment, one of the claims articulated on the selective precipitation technology was exactly in the same way that we had thought of. It was a nervous moment for me. All of those lines suddenly became related to the project. It was an application with priority dated back to 2013 when we had already developed the concept and had a few experimental data from the lab indicating proof of the concept. We had thought of a quick publication in a journal as mentioned by Dr Gilbert. However, we were delayed over and over by the constant work pressure in the lab; busy in preparing project documents, stage gate notes and some funny excuses. Within a few days, I received a strange news that the same biotechnology company was offering demonstration trials of the technology to the European counterpart of our company.

"How smart they are to carry coals to Newcastle?" one of my colleagues, Mehak, asked in surprize.

I nodded, "Yes, we have delayed making it to public." It was not like the early days when the US patent law offered the first to invent criteria. We could not prove the date of the invention by producing our lab note books, other documentation and claim for an earlier priority date. A PCT application does not mean that it would come out as a granted patent in designated countries. However, I did not find any strong reference cited against the claims by the patent examiner in his report mentioned in the last page.

We tried to play with the cat without trying to bell it properly and had no idea when someone else had belled the cat inside the dark room. "We were delayed," "we were careless"—all these phrases were meaningless to us as we could not reverse the time. I shared the reference with Dr Gilbert.

"I will contact our in-house IP attorney." He sounded a bit casual to me. I gathered some thoughts in the meantime. What could have been done better to avoid this situation in future? What was the lesson?

Wise men think alike

Idea generation is an important aspect of the industrial R&D. It is very true that the competitors trying to address a specific problem will think in a similar way and sometimes even in the same way. Probably one among all the others will prove the concept and others will leave the idea to work or eventually may end up with re-inventing the wheel. A few smart inventors could design around it and get through with improved inventions. Some will try to bell the cat in the darkness. Some will try to hold the cat and let it out to public early. Some will try to harness a smarter cat, learning from their competitors. The game goes on.

I used to hear a phrase from the technical people: "Learn to think differently." Does this sound a cliché? I asked myself how it is possible. All the average intellects think alike and, if thousands of scientists work on a problem, probably many of them will end up with the same solution. Some of them will have different solutions. A few of them will have unique solutions. Very few will end up with patentable inventions which are fit for the purpose. There is always a risk that you could not grab the cat on time, even though you are a very efficient planner. A quick publication of your invention is one way to ensure that no one else could file the patent. However, you must grab the cat in the dark room and take it out to daylight quickly. The risk for playing with a cat in the dark is that someone else can bell it before you can come out of the room with it.

The Barren Lands

I refer to the battle field mentioned in previous chapter. The mines are planted sporadically and you wish to find a barren land to stand, position yourself in the battlefield and operate safely. One way is to search and ensure that no mine is planted near you and you can feel safe. However, it's not a safe haven forever. With the progress of time, there is a possibility that some "efficient" and more "improved" devices could be planted in your so-called "barren land." Even in some instance, during your search and zeroing-in of the land, someone may sneak in with a device. So, your haven is not safe anymore. How you can stand, plan an ambush and retaliate when you feel that the soil under your feet is not safe? The question is, how does one secure a firm grip. How does one ensure a "freedom to practice?" How does one minimize the risk down to an appreciable level?

The "freedom to practice" search is the most critical and difficult search for an IP analyst. I wish to mention that this is not a one-time practice for a client. It is a surveillance practice needed to be performed again and again with time. You could always expect your sniffer dog to smell a foul every now and then.

The chronic unease

I heard of the "Gilbert syndrome" for the first time when I visited my general physician at Bangalore. Gilbert syndrome refers to the absence of some enzymes in detoxification metabolic cycles in the liver. Due to some enzymes being less active or absent, the situation gives rise to an elevated bilirubin level in blood. This is not a disease. This is a congenital description—a situation of the state. However, it creates a chronic unease in the body. The statement like, "We would quickly publish our invention and will secure a freedom to practice" sounds like a Gilbert syndrome. At that moment, I felt weak and the sentence initiated an unease in my brain.

Another idea shared long ago by my sniffy friend Ankur, "Let's gather some lapsed patents, those which still have some business importance, and just think of practicing some of the inventions." It sounded very logical in my early days, in 2005. I was in tutelage of all my senior colleagues and all the suggestions and advice I received from them, I took for granted without a second thought. However, down the timeline, I am in doubt if Ankur would reiterate his sentence with same confidence. If the scope of the original older invention is broad and someone in the future claims a significant improvement of the properties for a segment or a subset, then there is ample chance that the application could be granted as a patent. Sometimes, the patenting process is like a demon's blood dripping out of its throat and, the moment it touches the ground, a hundred new demons are created. One invention gives rise to another within the scope of the same or germinates nearby.

Quo vedis?

The freedom to practice is like playing with a fire. There is nothing wrong in it but you should know that you are playing with fire. At any time, you may end up with infringing someone's granted patent claim. The Gilbert syndrome is not a disease but I need to know whether I have the Gilbert syndrome. The sniffer dog should stay alert at the battlefield. The best way to ensure freedom to practice is probably to file a patent and get it granted, if possible. If it's not granted because of the same invention mentioned in a lapse patent or in journal literature as cited by the patent examiner, you have more reasons to be happy. You have performed a due diligence. Although it would not ensure your practice right away, you could at least find yourself in a better strategic position in the battlefield. It would reduce the chronic unease. You can safeguard the barren land by ring-fencing yourself, keeping an ever-alert sniffer dog and letting the game continue.

The steps to secure the practice right:

1. A freedom to practice, search and analyze, to ensure that the process or the product does not fall

under the scope of any granted claim of living patent at a selected territory (country).

2. The best option of ensuring a freedom to practice is to file a patent application, if the process or product is novel and inventive, and law could permit a granted patent. If not, it still would end up with a patent publication in public domain.

3. As a second line of defence, publish the work in open literature/report as soon as possible. This is not a full protection for practice.

4. Repeat the freedom to practice search as an update on a regular basis to reduce the risk of infringement.

CHAPTER FOUR

The Sniffer Dog: Role of IP Analysts

Unfolding the story

It was late on a Monday morning. Gluing my eyes to computer screen, I was going through search results captured by the patent database with lazy eyes. My desk phone rang twice and I stretched my left hand to reach the cradle.

"Tarak... tea?" It was Srini. He perhaps came a bit late to the office. He must have reached Bangalore in the morning by an overnight train from Chennai, his hometown. I nodded to his call and, the moment I was about to leave my seat, my eyes spotted a recent patent application by our competitor. I scrolled down hurriedly to the "claim section" and read the first independent claim. I murmured in head, "Gaurav!" as I went through dependent claims as well keeping my breath held inside my lungs. I pressed the print button, ran to the nearest print machine and took off with a few loose printed papers. How long does it take to cover the distance from the second floor of the Pathfinder building to the ground floor of Pioneer? Perhaps a minute. I covered the same within 30 seconds at most.

Gaurav was getting ready for his lab. I caught him right at his work station. I fetched out the printed documents, "See the last but one page... the claims." He was engaged in some other thoughts and did not expect me to visit his desk at this hour.

He received it, took more than a minute to read and looked up. "You... again?" I clearly saw the disappointment in his eyes and could not bear his stare for more than a few seconds.

I slowly passed through the corridor and came down to Srini's desk. The man in his mid-fifties, with heavy glasses covering his eyebrows, was almost leaning over his desktop. He noticed my presence through the peripheral vision. Srini was my mentor for three years in my first organization. I came under his tutelage from day one when I misunderstood IP as short form of inter penetrating polymer type mechanism. Srini spoke in his husky voice as usual, "Wait for a minute,"

Neither was I ready to wait, nor had I the patience to hide the news further. I announced my arrival with a nervous voice, "I have killed another."

It made Srini transfer his attention from the screen to my face. I did not allow a few seconds to open his mouth. I started to utter each word slowly and separately, "I have found somebody who claimed the use of Methyl substituted terephthalic acid for amorphous polyester in a patent application."

Srini turned his chair completely towards me. A smile had found the narrow opening through his thick lips. I stayed there as a nervous student. He had now gathered some time to frame a sentence, "Don't be disappointed.

Perhaps you have correctly spotted a mine in the landscape. It helps the company to save the dollars!"

...Ears start to see, eyes listening!

The characters are fictitious, but the story is true. Two things are important for a business organization—either earning money or saving money. Sometime, the second one also becomes very significant. The role of an IP analysts is not only to search for and analyze the "patentability" of a possible invention but also he/she needs to remain black-and-white for decision-making. The IP attorney could rely heavily on the search/analysis carried out by a good and experienced IP analyst and thereafter can suggest the business to go ahead for patent filing or drop the idea. IP analysts often hold the sole command to move ahead in the patenting battle. He or she can sniff the gun powder, estimate the ground vibrations and help the entire technology team to move forward. A person with very good technical background could become a smart IP analyst, as they need to understand the technology after being trained in IP laws. The difference between a smart sniffer dog and the IP analyst in real world is that the dog only identifies the mines planted by the rebels, while an IP analyst points out the dangers as well as the vacant spaces to plant new mines (patents), which we call "white spaces" in our language. The role of an IP analyst starts even before R&D steps into a new battlefield. He/she draws a landscape with the mine locations in advance spots a few pieces of vacant, safe and target lands by talking to technologists and business. A good analyst searches for safe and potential *white spaces* in the landscape. However, a better analyst can scrutinize the first three mine locations (patent applications) of the competitor and can foresee the fourth one. Does this sound like *Hercule Poirot* in ABC murderers? Maybe. Moreover, a vigilant analyst keeps a surveillance on the field like a military dog at the frontier.

It's a balancing game

Gaurav did not look happy. There was no reason to be happy anyway. He was on the verge of collecting sufficient experimental data and already had filled up a request for patent application (RFPA). On that basis, I started a patentability search. He himself executed a preliminary prior art search and did not get the indication of any threat. I was not happy as well. However, if I did not mention that reference to business, it was almost certain that the patent examiner would pull this out during initial search or office action and it would have been hard for us to get through. As indicated in the previous section, an IP analyst could try to mark possible locations of mines in the technology battlefield. However, during early landscaping, there is every chance that he/she would have missed one or two here and there. This is particularly when there are Japanese and Chinese patent applications or some other non-English language countries where the full text of proper English translations is not easily available and there is a chance to miss something important. In some cases, even in the US and European patent applications, the abstracts and claims are written in uncommon technical terms and are difficult to get captured by keywords or structural (Markush) search. Nevertheless, it is still better if the *significant* reference is captured at last minute before the submission of applications. You could buy some more time to design around it, if possible, or abandon the application. Even if the reference is missed by the patent examiner (can't imagine such a lack of smartness) and the patent gets granted, there is a chance that patent infringement (pre- or post-grant opposition) could be filed by the competitor or by a third party. So, in this case, you have belled a cat who was already belled by someone earlier and the dispute would happen surely if the "cat" is valuable. What advantage do you get even if you pass through the examiner's eyes and get your patent granted? The harnessed cat was enjoying licking milk from the bowl and you have put another harness to it. So, it will not recognize you as the owner and protect your home from the mouse. You may end up with a granted patent without any freedom to practice. It's not wise to drain your energy to implant a mine with a faulty pressure sensor.

Story of a double belled cat

If a cat has two bells around its neck, then whose cat is it? The common perception is that the cat belongs to the person who belled it first. However, this common perception does not hold good in the patent field. A patent is an exclusive right. So, the "who has belled the cat first" excludes others from its ownership. The person who belled it next also excludes all others from ownership. So, the fun is that the cat does not belong to either of the two who belled it. They cannot "own" the cat any more unless both are ready to compromise and reach a mutual agreement. So, before trying to bell a cat or even harness it, you need to check if the cat does not have a bell around the neck or attached to any part of its body already. IP analyst could conduct a pre-check that you should not end up with a "non-bell-able" cat. In the IP field, this is called a "patentability" search and analysis.

No man's land

Perhaps it's getting a bit boring with cats and dogs. Suppose you are a civilian, not interested in a battle but you try to put up a patch of green in the war zone. How do your select your land? How to de-risk this from the under-earthed mines? Who will help you? You need to select a "no man's land" where nobody has planted any danger. A smart cat wishes to grab the fish without wetting its feet. Even if you are neither interested in filing a patent of the process or product you wish to commercialize, nor do you wish to know the patenting battle, still, you need to know that the "subject" of your process or product or the article has not been already captured (blocked) by any "alive" granted patent in the same territory (country). Even your belled cat excludes others from the ownership, it does not mean it is fit for grabbing fish without wetting its legs. This process of "de-risking" is called a search for "freedom to operate/practice" as explained in the last chapter. The practice right of a process/product is territory-specific and not directly dependent on whether you have a granted patent or not.

An IP analyst has to shift his/her mindset while looking for a freedom to practice from a patentability aspect. The patentability action is somewhat like creating a blockage or securing a terrain. This would not ensure the reaping of benefits from the invention. Rather, it would ring-fence your invention from possible intruders. The freedom-to-practice is the exercise to verify your process or product for practice rights. It does not matter if it is patented or not. It is commercially practicable without any legal implication.

Consider that you have an excellent invention. You have applied for a patent and ultimately got it granted. IP analysts ensured that, most probably, it would have the freedom to practice. After that, can you take it apart from the analyst? You do not need his/her help any more, at least not for this invention, right? Consider if another patent, granted in due course, partially or fully covers (rare though) your subject matter. Then what? The situation would be like the same as described in the last section "a double-belled cat." The only difference is that you would find yourself at the receiving end. Please remember that the analysts are like sniffer dogs. Their duty does not finish when the battle is over. The barren lands are still open for planting new mines—no one knows when and by whom.

CHAPTER FIVE

The Family Felidae: Evaluation of Patent Families

Dialogue at Damrac

"We need to take a call on that." Daisy did not seem happy to me but I could understand the subject matter she was referring to. I was a bit confused if a senior IP attorney like her, who is well-settled in a multinational, should be worried about that? After all, it is a business call. Yes, "we"—means the IP division—needed to understand the business. However, the question is, if we could sense that a joint venture will not offer us a good business in the long term from the point of view of IP, if we could (or we should) raise the flag?

It was a casual over-the-coffee meeting with Daisy at Damrac Square in the early evening and I thought that she would be in a hurry to catch the train for the north. I have seen the crowd at the Amsterdam Centrale in the evening and it is not a very different affair to catching a local train like we do in Kolkata. However, Daisy was lost in thought about the IP coverage of our joint venture partner, Agilegen. She started to frame her questions in the backdrop of the church with the noises of passing-by cars and trams on the main road. "You think that the kind of IP coverage they have is not going to lead us anywhere in future?"

I had a bite of my croissant which was sitting intact for the past five minutes on the plate, and replied "I think so."

I never thought of the consequence of this three-word reply on that chilly evening. I continued in a casual voice, "I have a feeling that we are lagging behind the competition as per the present patent portfolio held by our Agilegen."

Daisy finished her cup with a long sip, "I see. By the way, are you visiting the Dan Haag office on Monday morning?"

I stood up, thinking that we are ready to leave the Café. "Yes Daisy, we have a meeting."

Daisy was also about to leave. She placed her purse in the office bag and stepped up. "I have to run for my train. Anyway, meeting you at the office on Monday. By the way, it's getting very interesting!" Her eyes always spoke an additional sentence and, this time, it was more than the obvious. I left the place for my hotel room on the main road while she disappeared through the evening crowd towards the tramline.

Coming back to my tiny hotel room, I tried to gather my thoughts. It trickled down from the early-day technical conversation with Chris. We expected a perfect match of technology from our joint venture partner to what we were developing in-house. Chris had a feeling that our partner was not developing a robust technology; was not quick enough to respond to the market challenges. During a majority of the time, he was talking to me while facing the window. The penultimate question came to me as he turned his chair almost ninety degrees, "…and Tarak, what is your patent analysis is telling you? Anything new about them?" That was the start of the saga. I mentioned it all, in detail, to Daisy over the evening coffee. The partnership was indeed expensive—we bought almost half of the stake of Agilegen two years ago. If we decided to discontinue, we may face a "technology loss." If we continue with them, we may lose out in the race in the future. The question came to me again and again, "What is your patent analysis telling you?" How would I find an answer for that? How would I analyze a patent portfolio? Taking a step back, what were the parameters on which basis I could evaluate the patent portfolio of Agilegen?

I thought of an early dinner. I preferred to limit myself to a regular pizza and returned to the hotel room. The mattress was optimally cold to doze off. However, it could not reduce my consciousness. "What my patent analysis telling me?"

...It's the "Clowder of Cats"

Belling the cat is the process to obtain a granted patent, process to ring-fence your innovation, protecting it from others. However, if you have a few belled cats as well as a few cats yet to be belled, how would your situation look like? A few of the belled cats are very valuable, while a few of them are okay-ish. A few of them are doing the "cat walk" only. A few cats are yet to be belled but you have thrown lase by thinking those would be important and could provide a good business in the long term. Similarly, if a company has a group of patent applications in a specific technical domain, some of them would be granted; a few of them would be waiting for a grant; and a few would face tough challenges from examiners because of existing close prior arts. So, how would you compare the patent portfolio of one company to the other for a specific domain? It's all about evaluating a clowder over individual cats.

Someone back in the Bangalore office tried to put his head down to attempt this before. He thought it is the number game. The more the number of patent families you have, the richer is your portfolio. It does not make sense to me. It is hard to evaluate the patent portfolio without reading each of the patent families. If you find that hundreds of patent families belong to a company in a technical domain, it is a mammoth task to read them all—forget about the comparison task. The parameters on the basis of which a patent portfolio would be evaluated should be easily found out or calculated by the available patent search or databases on the internet. Only then can you do the evaluation and comparison of portfolios within a short time. We should look for the outlined features of the cat to understand or predict their behaviour. An attacking cat speaks about it through the eyes. We have no time to study individual behaviours and make a perfect analysis. The speed over the accuracy needs some assumptions to reach a near-perfect conclusion.

Evaluation... Family Felidae...

I was not a big lover of pizza but I felt an urgency to finish my supper and get to my hotel room. So, I decided to go down to the food outlet right opposite to my hotel and asked for the menu card. The waiter whispered, "We have several kinds of Italian delights but only a few of them matter. If you talk about the taste!" Yes, only a few of them matter and that's why the customers hang around there for a while. It was quite evident from the common plates placed for orders. I got my answer, only a few… those are all that matter. How could I find those few? I left my last bite on the plate and went up to the room and started scribbling on a piece of paper.

The "number of patent families" is obviously important. Then comes the number of granted patent families (at least one member is granted). The granted patents mean that an effective fraction of those are ring-fenced and are supposed to do the business. They are followed by an average number of years that remain to expiry per family. After all, a young clowder gets more time for haunting! Another important parameter can be the average number of countries filed by patent families. This is probably the individual business decision but, if the subject matter is of worth, the company should have tried more countries to protect their innovation. Some technology is country-specific. We need to be careful. Another parameter may be the number of average forward citations. If the patent families have more value, they would be cited by the others in future. However, it could be a misguiding factor if the technical area is new or it is a new entity in the market. I jotted down a few more points with explanations in brief. The next part of the job was to allocate the weightage to each parameter and it took me almost till midnight. I was about to hit the bed. While turning off the lights, I murmured, "My patent analysis has started talking now."

Making a decision

The seminar room at Den Hague was big enough to host about fifty people. I recall there were about six patent analysts and the rest was a group of attorneys and business analysts. I asked Vernon, the senior council, "How much time do I have?"

He seemed uncertain to me, but replied, "Maybe a half an hour to forty. You can wrap up by then." I started my presentation in silence. As I started to narrate the evaluation of parameters and weightages, lots of debates and counter arguments popped up. When I was about to finish my last slide, I glanced to my wristwatch. It had crossed almost two hours. Although I thought all the questions were asked and the room was flooded with arguments and counter-arguments already, still I looked up and uttered, "If you have any more questions…"

A firm voice spoke out from the first row, "So now is the time to decide whether we should continue with Agilegen or put a full stop?"

The business lead, Philippe was sitting at first row and holding his chin all through. I could not guess whether he had listened to me for the entire time or not. I was not sure what to answer, so tried to clarify, "Do you wish to know my opinion?"

He did not remove his palm from his chin and replied, "Yes."

I did not notice this but an instant question came out from my mouth. "How much time do I have?"

He stared at me and lifted up his left hand and checked his wrist watch. "Five minutes."

Five minutes was short. In fact, it was too short. It was the time to grab a coffee, respond to a bio-break and come back within the conference room. Still, to this day I cannot recall if I had more than a minute's time to collect myself and decide. Moreover, I was confused about how a patent portfolio evaluation exercise for a group of competitors, including our joint venture, could lead to an important business decision. Phillipe was in a hurry and asked me straight way, "Is it a yes or a no?" He was too precise. He did not allow me to escape through any narrow openings. I was left with nothing. Nothing to formulate a sentence, nothing to even form a phrase. I only said, "No." There was no single question thereafter. No argument broke through. Philippe stood up and announced, "Let's stop here and move out. We are delayed for lunch."

The flight back to home...

The Flight to Charles de Gaulle on Saturday morning was delayed by a half an hour. So, I needed to spend some more time at Schiphol terminal. After the security check, I sneaked in and sat down in the lounge. A brown coloured newspaper was lying idle at the side of my table. As I unfolded the first page, a white page from middle portion of the newspaper fell on the floor. The business page of *The Guardian* had its headline: "…decided to terminate joint venture with Agilegen."

I carefully dropped the page into my hand luggage and started to walk down towards the boarding gate. "Yes… A few all those matter."

CHAPTER SIX

The Cat Has Nine Lives: Smart Patenting

To be or not to be...

"...We need to file the patent application." It was an obvious voice from Srinivasan. He paused, cleared his throat twice and then continued, "The question is what do we need to protect and how?"

The dilemma was that we were often not sure of how to describe the invention. We consider that the patenting process is to bell the cat and, more precisely, the "right" cat that suits our purpose. We know that we need to bell a cat. However, there is a need to define and select the cat which we are to bell. Otherwise, there can be a mismatch between the size of the knot, the dimension of the bell, and so on. With respect to the cat and not making these all right at first go, we may eventually lose the cat. Srini was playing with his computer mouse as his index finger was busy moving the roller up and down. "The cat and mouse game is not all about catching the mouse. The process starts with selecting the right and appropriate cat that can serve the purpose."

We knew that we had an invention. However, it was important to define the invention. Sometimes, the inventors himself is lost in thought or in scientific details and cannot define invention correctly. I recall someone who, in the invention disclosure form, started writing,

"The invention involves…" and Srini almost pounced on the paper.

"An Invention is an invention. It cannot involve or get associated with anything. If you can't define an invention in a single sentence, it's not an invention at all." Yes, after fifteen years, I can rewrite each word of the sentence he has uttered. If you cannot define your cat properly, that means it is not the right time to decide on filing an application. It may need some more data, clarity and discussions. A good patent analyst is a sniffer dog who should be very clear about the blacks and whites. If a decision needs to be taken whether the invention has been properly defined or not, the response should come with either *yes* or *no*. There is no scope for dilemma, provided that any other technical or business reasons hold this back.

Catch a healthy cat

During my first discussion with my mentor, he asked me "What is a claim?"

I started in a tentative voice, "The claim involves the protection…"

He stopped me then and there itself and did not allow to complete the sentence. He cleared my confusion in the first go, "The claim is the invention."

Later, I learnt that the heart of the patent application is the "first independent claim." So, defining the "invention" is very important. A healthy cat can catch many mice (businesses).

Catching a healthy cat is a team game. The inventor needs to define the cat. The IP analysts and attorney could help and suggest. This is not only the first step towards the patenting process, but probably the most critical step. On this basis, the claims would be construed; examples and comparative examples would be required to support the claims. Even one step ahead, smart claims may be construed. If not all, at least it triggers the thought process. In the voice of one of my sniffer dog buddies, "The invention should be mentioned as specifically as it is possible so that we can claim it as broadly as it is permissible." The inventor needs to show the spot, define the spot in the war field; the sniffer dog will dig it out. This is the time where the IP analyst has the scope to search the inventiveness. Later on, when the claims are construed, he/she can go for a full-fledged patentability search and analysis. During the search operation for inventiveness, IP analysts could get an idea about the technology area, how crowded it is and how far the scope could be expanded.

More meat on the bone

Let's go back to the original question—how to catch a healthy cat? The cat itself will not appear healthy. Rather, we need to put more meat on its bones to make it a healthier one. The role of the IP analyst is to analyze the invention and the surrounding areas. He/she considers the data, examples and would judge how much broader a claim could be construed. If it is possible to broaden the claim, but the IP analyst and attorney think that there is limited data available to support the claim, then it is the inventor's responsibility to generate the required data. So, to make the cat healthier, the IP analyst and attorney serve as veterinarians while the inventor feeds it as per the direction. The more accurate the analysis and smarter the decision, the healthier the cat will be. It is also important to know this if at all we need to overfeed the cat. Does it mean, if the scope is there, we would broaden the claim even if it is not necessary?

Of course, we do not have to spend an extra penny for that unless the number of claims go higher and over the limit. When a patent application with broader claim coverage is granted, then it is worthy. We can feed the cat and make it tubby. However, there is an animal dietitian called "patent examiner" who always tries to make your cat "slim and trim." You and your patent attorney oppose and try to maintain the overweight cat. So, the tussle between the dietitian and your attorney continues, which is called "office actions" in patenting languages. The tussle ends with a compromise and the dietitian releases your cat with optimum weight or while underweight, whether you like it or not. However, the cat should be healthy and well fed at the beginning to withstand the torture of the dietitian! In whatever form the cat is released with a bell and lasso in your hand, you should accept that for mouse hunting!

Catwalk on the ramp

Some organizations used to bell only the cats those they needed to carry on with the cat-and-mouse game. This is very understandable. The patent application and getting those granted are meant for commercialization and as a business tool. However, as I said, some companies file patents in the areas not known as their core area of business and sometimes patents are filed far away from their war zone. It's hard to connect and understand the intentions where no immediate business interests are seen. So, those cats left in barren lands are not interested in catching mice and rather do a "cat walk." The objective is mainly two-fold. If any business interests originate to those areas, these patents could be utilized. So, the cats could forfeit their "inertness," leave the ramp and suddenly would become carnivorous. So, it is like a wait and watch game. The second reason may be to deviate the attention of the competitors or the market that the company is trying their business in new areas. Even though it is hard to understand the motivation. In patenting words, it is called "aggressive patenting." It is like releasing more cats without any estimation of the number of mice around only because you never want to lose out in competition. More number of cats would ensure that every mouse would be efficiently caught and will never allow your competitors' cats to go for happy hunting.

The cat with nine lives

A healthy cat that has been fed well by you, adequately vaccinated by a veterinarian and shaped by dietitian could be an asset. It has resilience against the odds (oppositions) and can be a good hunter (drawing business). This is not always true. The exception proves the statement of course! Even I have seen that a granted patent with very narrow claims can be a killer. A thin cat with higher concentration could focus more on a targeted mouse. If one construed a set of claims with narrow coverage fit for the purpose only with a very well-checked background, one may experience less time for office action. It could be granted in lesser time with lesser arguments (office actions). So, the cat could be on-the-job released at an early stage.

The cats of different attire and motivations are out in the field. Some are already on their business. Some are on wait-and-watch moods. Some cats demonstrate sauntering gestures. Choose your cat, the cat with nine lives. Happy hunting!

Apart from blocking others to practice, patenting an invention has other following objectives:

1. Covering more area in same technical field, even without any immediate intentional to practice.

2. Filling in the intermediate areas (white spaces) those are not covered by key patents.

3. Supporting a business moving to new technical areas.

CHAPTER SEVEN

Sniffer Dogs on Barren Land: The Importance of Provisional Application

Afternoon at Airoli

The lazy afternoon sun filtered through the rare window while I was going through Srijesh's invention disclosure. The subject matter was chemistry, which I had abandoned a few years ago in GE during my IP analyst job. It was like recapturing the nuance of polymer chemistry. The invention was about a process to prepare a cross-linkable polymer precursor. While I was reading, I realized that I had lost "touch" of Polymer Chemistry, which was my everyday bread and butter during my PhD days at IIT Kharagpur, almost 20 years ago. I was going through the pages for description and schematics quickly as the patent agent was in a hurry to file this provisional within a week. Interestingly, Srijesh was not in a hurry. At least I did not perceive such a pressure from him. Whenever I asked for any document and clarification, he used to acknowledge my mail and calmly reverted to me after two to three days without any rush. These kinds of clients are good in the sense that we could do our job with calmness and patience. However, a lesser pressure for filing from clients also makes IP analysts lazy dogs sometimes.

As I was going through the pages, my eyes stuck to the reaction schematic he had drawn. He told me earlier that it was a well-known molecule he had synthesized. So, the invention disclosure was about the process only. Out of curiosity (I feel some chemical bugs move around my brain whenever I read this types of disclosures), I started to draw the detailed schematic on my own. By the time the sun had completely set, darkness prevailed in my Navi Mumbai apartment at Airoli, and I stood up to switch on the light. Exactly at that moment, I realized that, as per Srijeesh's new process schematic, the reaction product was different. It was different from what comes out of the "known process." Although, this was about the existence of an additional methyl group in the structure, which was not possible if one followed the regular synthetic route. I had to leave my seat and stood up for another time to call Srijeesh. I wished to speak to that guy.

A sniffer canine

Planting a mine is a tricky game. What is trickier is how much area you would like to cover for your "plantation." It should not be more so that you ask for more trouble; not less, so that you miss a chance to protect your slice of battlefield. A sniffer dog—patent analyst—always looks for additional opportunities when given a job for novelty analysis. Yes, an inventor wishes to file a provisional application to file as soon as he gets an idea supported by some data. This is just to ensure a *date of invention*. However, an analyst should not be in a hurry to review an invention so that he would miss anything "additional" to include in disclosure. Yes, a provisional application is a kind of disclosure—a description of the "possible" invention that may contain any claim or not. However, this does not mean that it has less importance as a "quick file document." As the document /disclosure is written at the very early stage of innovation, a full-fledged patentability search is not possible. The opportunities are not identified yet. You are even not in a position to construe the claims, are you? An analyst could understand a bit from the nature of the invention and can assume what could be the form of a "developed invention" at a later stage. What is more interesting is the "assumption" part. It is a perception. A novelty search could be conducted on the basis of that perception that could be a probable reality when the non-provisional application would be filed within a year.

The role of a sniffer dog is not limited when you wish to select as much area as you try to cover within your reach. It is not harmful until and unless you physically step into the barren lands (filing a non-provisional application). Later, if your smart canine sniffs a danger, you could refrain from planting your mines.

Say "YES!"

When the subject of a provisional application is a new process, the new process could lead to a product or mixture of products. The product may be known or there is a chance that it is barely different from the prior art. It may or may not have sufficient efficacy. The art is to realize this and incorporate the information in the disclosure. Sometimes, at the initial stage of writing the disclosure, we may not know if the product (or the mixture of products) is the novel or not. Moreover, very less time is available to search for that. Even a quick search for novelty could be inconclusive. In such a situation where you have the options either to go or not to go, it is always better to go. This is because, the corresponding non-provisional application always provides a chance to "drop" the added features, but will not allow you to include anything new. A provisional application will allow you a year to search if the "product" is novel, how you could support the "enhanced efficacy" and collect or generate the evidence. In parallel to consolidating the data related to the process, we could testify the product and differentiate the "known art." A provisional application is the first and last chance to plant additional mines in the battlefield. The non-provisional application is like the consolidation. You may carefully choose and justify what to consolidate and what you need to leave behind. A provisional may be a dream and a non-provisional will bring that to reality—at least some part of the dream.

Bell a Cat or bell the kittens too?

It is not permitted to add anything new to the non-provisional application that did not exist or was not included in corresponding provisional application (out of scope). In that case, one needs to file a fresh application with a new date. The question is, if the inventor needs to wait until he gets considerable information to file a provisional or file a quick provisional application based on the existing information and anything left behind that could be added in form of another non-provisional application if needed. It's risky sometimes since the original non provisional application could be cited by the patent examiner as "prior art" to the other one with added information. If the kitten is looking similar (but not the same) to its mother, it is considered that the kitten carries the characteristics of its mother. So, you cannot bell the kitten anymore because you already belled its mother. If the kitten is not significantly different, then you lose a chance to bell the kitten. Rather, the examiner sometimes could suggest that there is more than one invention covered in a single patent application and the other part should be applied as a separate patent application. It is like a pregnant cat carrying its baby and is considered as two entities. After delivery (examiners advice), you could bell both kitten and mother as you have asked to bell the mother cat earlier. The both non provisional applications could carry the same priority date. However, not discovering the independent kitten early could be a problem. There comes the role of a patent analyst—to build a ring-fence around a provisional application itself by sometimes assuming that the mother-like kittens are around; and to arrange for the bells (additional area coverage). If the kittens could not be found readily at the time of the provisional application, one should leave the door open for it! If there is already a hint that such a kitten exists, then that needs to be considered for belling.

For Srijesh, we had arranged a bell and defined a broader scope for the provisional application (defined a tubby cat?). Srijesh had a year to consolidate and prove the product composition with the additional function anticipated. It also could help him prove that his synthesis process is "significantly different" ,unique and he could possibly claim the product composition, too.

CHAPTER EIGHT

Alone in the Battlefield: The Story of An Individual Inventor

Afternoon call

The telephone rang in my bedroom for a long time. I was reluctant to attend the call in the lazy afternoon of June. A continuous drizzle made the ring further inaudible. I finally managed to pick that up on time and discovered the screen showing a ten-digit number—meaning, it's from an unknown number. I cautiously started, "Hello?"

"Is that Dr Gupta on line?"

"Yes, speaking."

"Hello. I am Sharad Mund, speaking from Bangalore. I got your number from Sudip."

This made me completely volatile in mind, "Which Sudip?" I could not recall his last name. "However, he told me to contact you. Actually, I have some idea. I wish to patent it and so he directed me to you."

My drowsiness left me in a second as I started talking to the stranger who, what I perceived from his voice, was around fifty.

"I have an idea and I need to file a patent. Could you help me with that?" He was so straight in the face. The urgency was very prominent and he was caught in a jiffy such that if he could not file a patent he was going to lose the world. I find that quite interesting. I tried to make it a bit clear, "Lets meet face to face this weekend and talk." I felt that the conversation over the phone was not the right way. Moreover, if I need to deal with a client, I should arrange a non-disclosure agreement first.

The gentleman agreed for next Saturday at CCD at Indiranagar. Though it is a bit far, I thought I could manage weekend traffic.

Entering the minefield

It is not the same when you look into the possible filing of an innovation by an organization and that by an individual. The risk is manifold. An organization excelling in a specific technical area is aware of the possible competitions and the possible risk of placing feet on unearthed mines. However, when an individual inventor comes up with an isolated idea, mostly with no data, I am not sure whether this would work or not or has any practical application. Moreover, the inventor carries a false assumption that, if he or she gets a patent, he could start practicing or selling his innovation and earn a lot of money, it's a whole other ball game. Many a times, I have needed to arrange a "calm down session" and manage the expectations. The issue with individual inventors is that each one premeditates that "I need a patent." If I ask him/her "why do you need a patent?" the answer comes back as "I have an idea (you would rarely hear about the word "invention"), so I want to get a patent and sell the process or product." I used to frame the next question, "Why do you need to file a patent for selling your product?"

Now the client would get irritated sometimes, "Because, by obtaining a patent, only I have the "license" for the product or process and no other person can do it." Now this puts me in trouble. Several questions pop up in my head and I remain perplexed which one to fire first?

Do you have an "idea?" Why do you think that it is "an invention?"

If it is an invention, do you have sufficient data to support it? If you do not have it, are you sure that you could generate the data that would support your invention or "new idea?" (workability)

If you get a patent granted even, I am sorry that will not assure you or give you the license to practice, produce or sell your process or product.

The last point usually leaves them blank. Just like a freeze-shot in a fiction movie.

Defining a space

The saga starts at the beginning. What is an invention? Usually the client starts with an explanation, "my invention is about this and that, involves mixing it with this and which is attached to that." Too many words sometime leave me blank as well. Long ago, my mentor told me, "If the invention cannot be explained in a sentence, then it is not an invention." I obey this guideline. The challenge in the first step is to get that sentence scanned out intact from the client's mouth. It is the first barrier. If this process goes wrong, then it will bring a disaster and ruin all diligent works in next steps. It is like a physician desperate to know the source of the problem while patients are blabbering about their pains and discomforts. Many a times, I found that the "invention" stays at a completely different location from what I presumed from the first few conversations with the client. Sometimes, I take the way of the eye physician too. While I am made to sit and look into a mirror reflection of different sizes of alphabets, she very patiently changes one piece of glass with another with slightly different power or cylindrical orientation and asks me very politely, "Is this better or earlier one?" If my answer creates any doubt in her mind, she repeats the step again asks the same question. Sometimes, she changes the sequences of altering glasses and asks the question, "Is this not better?" I know I get confused sometimes but, by repeating this process over and over again, she gets the answer—what exactly is my eye's condition at present that needs to be corrected with glasses. In the same way, I need to do this with the clients.

The Client Interview

Mr Mund, a middle-aged man fully dressed in business attire, was sitting opposite to me on that Saturday afternoon. He introduced himself as a chartered accountant and did not hesitate to mention that he is quite away from science and technology. "I am not into applied sciences but I have visited a customer's place for audit just a few months ago. Along with the technical team, the manager was accompanying us for a workshop tour. I was not interested in the production process details, but got interested when they showed us a big weighing machine which is supposed the weigh the raw materials. The balance was very big but very precise and it can read in milligram levels. However, I have seen that every time the person weighs the powdered materials, they add some part of it very carefully when it nears to the required weight. Sometimes, if he adds a bit more material in last part of the addition, it may lead to surplus and the operator needs to manually take out some materials from the pan. It's a laborious process, isn't it?" He stopped as the waiter was placing two medium cups of cappuchino on our table. I picked up the cup without touching the sugar cube. A minute later, he dropped one into his cup and started mixing that with spoon.

I asked him, "So, what is your idea here?" I was thinking about my masters and under graduate chemistry labs where we needed to follow the same process. If the settling time of the weighing balance was long, it would take more time to weigh the material.

Mr Mund answered, "I have an idea that if I could put a sample holder at the top of weighing machine and press the option panel with the amount of material I need to weigh, the system could dispense the exact weight of material on the weighing pan." Obviously, we needed a software to guide the automated process. By that time, I finished half of my cup and placed it on the table.

"So, do you have any idea how this could be done. I mean, for auto-dispensing the required amount/weight of material?"

He responded with a thought, "I don't know. This may be the task of a system engineer but how is my idea?"

The actual question between his lines was, "I need to get a patent on this idea. Could you do that?"

A Hanging Palace

Building a palace in the sky is not a bad idea at all but we need to consolidate the pillars attached to the ground very quickly. I have heard this somewhere. An idea with possible technical application is good but there is a need to explain how the idea will work. The workability of the idea may be a patentable invention. A patent cannot be granted on the basis of a mere idea. How does one convert the idea into reality, step-by-step, with logics? You may or may not have experimental data in the beginning, but there is a need to generate those steps, even before the need to search for a novelty. Is this a new idea? If not, how would the existing arts talk about the materialization of the idea?

I started to explain to him the process of getting a patent. Starting from the novelty, inventiveness, workability and applicability I narrated the conditions to obtain a granted patent. Then, I explained a journey from patent drafting, application till the grant of the patent. It seemed like Mr Mund was not very convinced.

I have come across many people who go by their own logic and think that a patent is all about filing an idea. It's a source of getting a license and earning money. A more confusing wish comes from some business or marketing professional who says, "I want to file an IP." That leaves me confused. What needs to be filed—a patent, a design, a trademark or a copyright? Why is this is needed to be filed? IP is like entropy. Every new idea, new research, technical information and art work is a different form of IP and its ever-increasing volume. However, any new idea is not patentable. Sometimes, we do not need to file a patent, even if it is a patentable invention. Some companies keep the invention as a "secret." Sometimes, ensuring the freedom to practice is enough to serve the business' purpose. Even an open publication would protect your interest to practice without applying for a patent.

Mr Mund agreed that he would revert to me after he "consolidates" his idea. While I was ready to start my car, I was pretty sure that he would never come back. I was smiling a bit while driving. At least the coffee was good.

CHAPTER NINE

Tail That Wags the Dog: The Claim Language

Someone interested

There was another evening call from my ex-office colleague. I was wondering whether it was related to any water or analytical need or just was a "Hi and hello." Normally with those who are not in touch on a regular basis, I get curious. However, Manikandan is a nice guy with a good analytical hand. Every time we discuss some chemical analysis process or instruments, I learn. I picked my headset. Mani is a calm guy. He never jumped to the discussion topic at the beginning. This time, it was the same. I was wondering and searching for the topic. He was slow to break the shell, "Do you know the very thin guy working in analytical chemical division in our office?"

It did not ring a bell for a few seconds. I was trying to recollect the thin and thinner. Then, it suddenly popped up—a figure with blue jeans and an unshaved face. Mani did not wait for my reply this time. "Shankar has some invention. He has found a natural resource to convert to alcohol."

I replied "great."

The next sentence was expected, "Do you know any patent agent who could draft and file his patent?" I did not ask any more questions to Mani. As he was not an inventor and Shankar probably would have shared the minimum information with him, there was no use of enquiring further. I just shared the contact number of my friend, Basu, who is a patent agent and thought that he could take care of this well. Usually, my job ends with sharing the phone numbers and, after a few days, I forget everything about the call and discussions. I did not come to know the outcome or fate of the project. Whether the patent application was drafted or filed, whether any issue appeared, remains unknown to me unless the inventor or patent agent gives me a call.

Did I bell the cat?

The phone came after a week when I was middle of my dinner. The first call was from Shankar who wanted me to look into the claim drafted by the agent. He wanted me to listen to him talk of his invention and wished me to look into the claim. I insisted him to sign a non-disclosure agreement first, then I would listen and look into anything. He was not very happy about this and asked me if it was really required. When I insisted, he agreed. After the NDA part was over, he called me again the next day and shared the set of claims already drafted by the patent agent over e-mail with a "confidential" mentioned in the subject matter. I opened the mail and went through all 10 claims one by one. It was about synthesis of wine from a natural resource by fermentation other than grape. The first thing that struck my mind was claiming, "A process to synthesize alcohol by adding…" Now my question was, how could I define an alcohol? Are we sure only an alcohol was formed? A natural fermentation or fermentation in the home environment may generate a group of compounds such as mono- or poly-hydroxy compounds along with alcohol and it could get mixed with unreacted sugar, carbohydrates and other materials in the final composition. Without going into detail in chemistry, I had doubts.

"Are we missing something here?" How would the patent examiner perceive this claim? If a process to synthesize alcohol was the right claim, could we go with a combination of possible compounds along with alcohol? The challenge was to bell the cat properly, otherwise there was every opportunity that the invention could be hijacked. Leaving it in the hands of examiner to decide was not a good option. Claim language is of utmost importance in the patent filing process. It defines the quality. If something is missed or not addressed properly, you leave a gap and another fresh application from a third party could look over your shoulder.

There is a sip

Shankar was not interested in a provisional application. We placed the option that we could file a provisional application and down the timeline; he could work upon to improve his invention. However, he mentioned that the competition is tough in the technical area and he wished to place the card as soon as possible. The challenge of belling the cat directly is the "preparation." If you are ready with the data to support the invention, then non provisional application would be the right way to proceed. The cat needs to be defined, assessed well, and then be pushed to a corner, ensuring that you covered all ends. Only then, the cat should be belled. By chance, if you leave a space, the cat could have an escape route. You thought that you belled "something," but it may not turn out to be the cat you wanted. Someone else could bell the cat as well.

Defining the product composition is critical. What is more challenging is the question of how to define the composition in the claim. It is not about claiming what you want and rather about what has been produced. The claim should consider all the possible products, if not already analyzed. If the product composition was not analyzed and you sense that there is a gap, it is better to go for a provisional application. Belling the cat early is not a wise option always. Particularly for individual inventor, the enthusiasm remains high and often moves by the emotions. In this case, Shanker was a bit restless. He thought that mentioning alcohol as the product would provide him the business edge. A patent is not a tool for advertisement. It is a techno-legal document. If the claims are not construed properly, either the examiner would raise objections or a new patent could make an entry into the scene. The examiner could cancel the claims if the inventor could not provide support to his claim. The claim is everything in a patent application. It is supported by the data, examples and comparative examples mentioned in the body. Any error in other portion of the patent application still could be rectified or overlooked, but the claim is the invention. If not construed properly, it could cost you later. The sincere suggestion would be to follow the sniffer dog. The wagging of the tail explains everything. It defines the state of mind and attitude. In same way, a claim tells everything about the patent.

This game of measuring the cat is important and so is arranging the bell of an appropriate size. If the cat is sensitive, there is a need to be more careful when designing the bell.

Walk like a cat on eggs

We need to take additional care while filing a patent for an individual. The objective for an individual inventor is to secure the invention and look for monetization in a short period. Hence, an IP analyst should analyze the claims very carefully and always keep in mind the maximizing of the business opportunity for the client. Any mistake or flaw in claim-construction may lead to rejection by the patent examiner and could lead to a heart break for the individual inventor. For organizations and companies, a patent filing may be a new addition to the existing patent portfolios. However, for an individual or sole entrepreneur, a single patent application may be the first step of initiation of a business arising out of a hard-earned invention. The cat is precious here. We need to ensure that the entrepreneur should not lose this by any chance. An extensive background (prior art) search, analyzing the claims drafted by patent agent and revising it several times, could secure the interest. A proper de-risking before the patent application is filed, could ensure the grant of patent in later stage. A kitten that is fed well could mature into a healthy cat.

Two years later

Shankar was happy to announce that his patent application was published. However, the real battle started there. The examination report was shared with inventor by the patent office with a lot of remarks asking for clarifications. Some questions were asked to clarify the claim language. The sniffer dog's job was not over yet. It was needed to find the references, arrange the data, correct the information and, most importantly, justify the claims to help the attorney respond to office actions. It needed to start a fresh journey—a journey to secure the place in the battlefield which was safe and strategic at the same time. The role of the sniffer dog is important before the submission of the patent application and after as well.

CHAPTER TEN

Set the Cat Free: When Not to File a Patent

I reached office just on time. Traffic during office time in Mumbai is terrific! For me to travel from Airoli to Turbe was merely 12 kilometres but, with traffic, it was almost uncertain to reach on time, even though I started 15 minutes early. I turned the AC on, settled in my cabin and opened my laptop. As I opened my outlook, I found an email sent by our CTO, Dr Phillip Gasbeek, the previous night from Switzerland. I opened the mail and glanced through hurriedly. The first sentence itself hit my brain very hard. "I suggest not to initiate a patent application for this filter design you have made last week." I started to read line by line now. He explained that the filter design to avoid dirt and particles as well as to delay the filter clogging was good but not a candidate for patent application. I was surprised. What was wrong with him and what was wrong with the design? As a technologist, I thought that I would put forward my invention disclosure by this week. It would have been my first success in this company. What annoyed me more was that Phillip did not justify the "decision." As I was doing a double hatting, I also analyzed my invention very thoroughly. I did not find any prior art (existing reference) to that design and it was a patentable "invention" as per the half of my brain. I lost my interest in the tea served by Ranamma. I was staring at the cup placed on the table, slowly losing heat by the cool air continuously getting dispensed from the AC vent. I looked into my mobile to check the time. Although it was very early in the morning in Zurich, the CEO of the company, Rajeev, would have been out of his bed as he was an early riser. I thought for a few second and initiated a WhatsApp call.

Rajeev normally starts the conversations with a single word, "Yes?" No hi, hello or good morning. I started talking slowly while explaining about the e-mail and my patentability search outcome. He was patient and listened to me all through. After I stopped explaining everything, he started, "It's a collective decision of the management. Do you think we are securing any business advantage by filing this patent application? I would like you to think for some time and call me back in the evening, I will again listen to you."

As I disconnected the call. Soheli knocked my office door. She was leading a microbiology team of our Mumbai R&D. She came to meet me quite earlier than other days. I presumed the reason would be some issue with the culture report of the inoculated water samples we had submitted to her the day before. She just opened the door slightly. I could only see her eyes and some part of her face. "What about your patent application?" I reluctantly responded by a single word "abandoned."

Set the cat free

In past, I used to do double hatting. I had the technical role as well as the IP analyst role at the same time for the organization I worked for. Since my research days in IIT, the technical part of my brain assessed the importance on patent filing, that is a sheer exaggeration. When I talk to other IP professionals, they are very keen and clear. If there is an innovation, go for a patent application. There are two advantages. If patent is granted, the innovation is secured and everyone else is blocked from practice. If it is not granted, then at least the invention would be published and no one else can file a patent. Not filing a patent would lead to an industrial secret within an organization. If secrecy is not "secured," or there is a "leak of information," then this could turn out to be a business threat. Now, let me put some devil's advocacy in favor of "not filing a patent." As a technologist, patent filing requires an initial allocation of the fund. If the patent does not get granted, there is no more expenditure after "request for examination" (u/s 11-B Indian patent act). However, if the patent gets granted, then it incurs recurring expenses every year for maintaining the patent right (grant status). However, these justifications do not hold well enough if the subject matter of the invention is in a highly competitive area where a company strategically or desperately tries build a portfolio to secure their business. However, if the company evaluates that the "importance" of the subject matter of the patent application is not very "business critical," then it can choose not to file a patent. Yes, to ensure the non-exclusive practice right, the company could publish the invention in the form of an open report or journal publication.

The patenting process is belling the cat in the dark room. The moment the cat is brought out of the room in open daylight, no one can bell the cat. To bell the cat or not to bell the cat is a business decision. The situation for institutions without any a direct connection to the industry is that they do not have the scope to "evaluate" the invention—if it is worth it to block the practice right (by filing a patent) or to publish in a journal (make it public and no longer patentable for anyone else). So, either of the instructions play an offensive approach. Either they file almost everything or they do not want the fund to drain and publish everything in a journal or in the form of an open report. When I was a PhD research scholar in IIT Kharagpur, I had a very limited idea about the patent rights. My worry was that, if my PhD research guide would have selected some other part of my work and he decided to file a patent, I would have lost more time to complete the thesis. I could not publish that subject in some esteem journal that could give me an advantage to apply for post-doctoral positions overseas. I had to wait till the patent application was filed in the patent office with a date of application (priority date). However, after more than 20 years, I realized that the patent application we put forward during my research days was not "necessary."

A few points I would consider before filing for a patent application:

1. If the subject matter or the invention is business critical. Is it related to a competitive growing market?

2. If the invention has a significant advantage over the existing arts.

3. If there is any immediate business need.

4. If the invention would provide any significant technical or cost benefit with respect to existing art.

5. If the "invention" in the application is really patentable. (Did the analysis suggest the subject matter as patentable?)

If the answers to many of the questions posed above are "no," I would not recommend a patent application. However, in those days, we had a limited source of information on the subject called "intellectual property" and we had to follow the institutional practice.

I do not know why

I was checking LinkedIn almost every day once. More than to check any message from contacts, I was interested in the new articles on water separation science. My eyes were glued to a recent post by my ex-colleague, Prerna, where she mentioned that her patent application was granted, which was originally filed from IIT Bombay during her PhD days. I wrote a congratulatory note in the comment section and continued to scroll. Meanwhile, over WhatsApp, I asked her about the subject matter of the patent. As I replied to the post, I was curious to know what prompted her to apply for a patent. As she had a granted patent in her kitty, what did she understand about the patent right?

She replied, "I need to ask my former PhD guide." This is perhaps the real representation of the situation in many universities and institutions. PhD students/researchers think that an addition of "patent" to their portfolio or resume would be an added advantage because it is a "superior" form of publication over the journal. I found that some of students have a misconception that, if their patents get published, it is done. They have no idea that a "granted patent" and the published form of patent applications are different. To publish a patent, you do not need to prove the novelty or technology feasibility. It is a published form of an unexamined and unchallenged literature and a publication in a journal literature stands better as the later goes through examination.

A one-liner in a resume, "A published patent application number... on..." does not add anything. Rather, it is meaningless. Many a times, institutes do not follow up after the patent applications and do not apply and deposit the fee for RFE (request for examination for Indian Patent u/s 11-B). So, the patent application does not get examined at all and becomes abandoned with time. If you bell the cat, you need to feed it regularly (read: RFE, annual fee for patent, fee to respond to office actions). If you fail to feed it, the cat will leave and you cannot block others to take away the cat, even though no one can bell it anymore. In some cases, even if the examination is requested and ultimately an application gets granted, the institute deposits an annual fee for the first year, only or for another year maximum. After that, the granted patent becomes lapsed. By that time, the student (inventor) is awarded the degree and leaves the campus for a job or post-doctoral research. If there is no industrial technology buyer foreseen (business drive) or immediate application, why does a researcher need to spend this much of time, money and effort? That is why primary knowledge in intellectual property is required for research students as well as for their research guides.

Non patent form of publication: A strategy

Yes, you got it right. Even not filing a patent for an invention is an essential part of the strategy for a patent-savvy industry. If the subject matter of the invention is not too business critical and there is no significant advantage to block the competitors, a company can go for a report or publication without any patent application. If the invention is merely incremental with respect to existing art, and the chance of getting a granted patent is feeble on the context of "obviousness" (Indian Patent Act u/s 3(d)), the business can decide not to go for a patent and save time and money. The patenting process, "belling the cat," is an art form. However, releasing the cat without belling it also a part of the game. Here, a good patent analyst comes into the picture. A sniffer dog assesses the risk and decides. Planting the mines only at some strategic locations is important to secure the footholds.

The evening call from Zurich

At post the lunch session, I was trying put myself in Philips' shoes. What made him decide not to file a patent on new filter design? I probably found some answers:

1. The new design was not too different from the existing designs available in market.

2. The advantage is there, but that is not proven to be "significant" to add value to the user and business.

3. We could wait for next version of filter design that may have a greater advantage and could qualify for "enhanced efficacy" as per the Indian patent act u/s 3(d).

4. If at all we secure a granted patent, it would take about three years from the filing as earliest. By that time, perhaps a more enhanced and smart design would be invented.

The last point is a "reality check." A patent application should be seen or projected as a future benefit. From the application to the granting, it would take some years. We cannot evaluate a patent on the basis of the market situation at present. We need to anticipate the future market. It is not easy to predict, particularly for a dynamic industry like water treatment, but for an analyst it is important to guess the competitive space in future. The technical knowledge blended with IP and business knowledge could help to take a decision.

Rajeev called me just before I was about to leave the office. This time, he did not start with a question or explanation, but in a different tone, "I know you have your answer by this time. Anything else I could help you with?" I replied with a thank you note and said bye. The call ended within a minute and I started my journey back home. Soheli was waiting for me at downstairs. As I went down, she said, "You looks happy! What happened?" I replied, "Yes, the IP part of my brain is happy and it is trying to pacify the other part of my brain." She was amused a bit, "Tarak, we may miss 6.28 train if we do not start right now." I smiled and replied "Sometime, missing something is good, isn't it?"

The Sniffer Dog

Decision making process for patent filing:
For Institutions/Researcher:

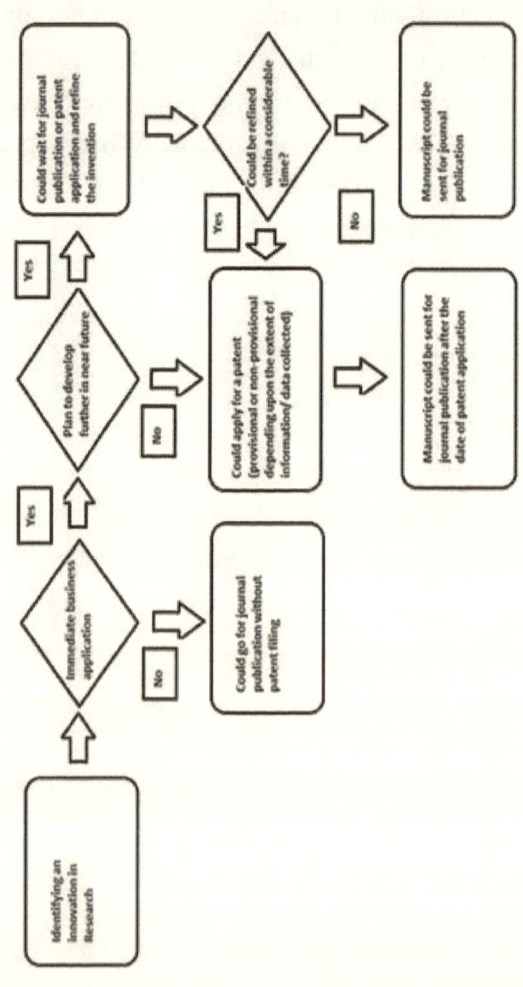

Decision making process for patent filing:

For Industry/Business:

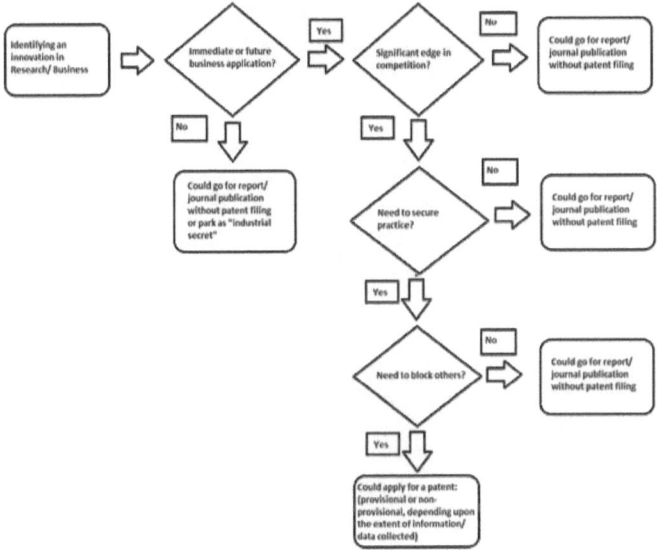

CHAPTER ELEVEN

All Cats are Grey in the Dark: Dilemma of Researcher

"Did you perform a thorough literature search earlier on the curing process of your ceramic material?" I asked Shantanu and I had to speak in a louder voice than normal as it was raining heavily and we were cycling side by side while we both were covered with rain coats. During our return from research lab at Materials Science in IIT Kharagpur, we usually used to drive bicycles very cautiously in the evening, particularly in the rain as we often found snakes were crossing the connecting roads. In the evening rain, it was hard to spot a snake amidst the fallen branches of trees and leaves. If anything, they would be moving very slowly on dark roads and were near impossible to spot in the insufficient light. I was unsure if those snakes were harmful or not but, many a times, the cycle tyres would skid over or hit a snake, falling down suddenly on the road was not a peasant experience.

Shantanu responded with a question without taking his eyes off the road ahead, "But why, G?" A few of the research scholars at BC Roy Hall used to call me by this nickname and Shantanu was one of them.

I replied without looking into him, "In case someone has already carried out the curing by the same process."

Shantanu was quick to respond, "If that had been the case, the examiners of my last two publications would have pointed it out, wouldn't they?" I nodded silently. During research days, we knew a patent publication was superior to a journal publication. But how and why? We had no idea. We did not realize on what grounds a patent gets granted. How the term "novelty" is associated with a patent? What is the better way to judge the novelty—securing a granted patent or a research publication in journal? We did not ask all these questions to our research guides. Not only Shantanu in ceramic lab, but I too did not bother to conduct a thorough literature search before moving deeper into my research projects. Once we wrote a draft for a journal paper and got it checked by our research guide, we would usually send it to a journal editor, depending upon the quality of the work and the subject area covered by the journal. After sending the manuscript, we waited for the days to receive a response. If the editor refused the manuscript without any examiner comment, or refused a manuscript based on examiners comment, we used to reformat the manuscript to make it suitable for another journal and resend. If the editor shared the examiners' comments, we needed to abandon our lab work for a few days to prepare the responses, got those checked by the research guide and sent the responses back to the editor. Once editor accepted the manuscript for publication, we were happy and celebrated what we thought was the "successful test" of our "novelty." Was not that so simple?

All cats are grey in the dark

Once the cats are out of the room, they all look similar in the dark. It is not easy to identify which cat is belled and which is not. If the cat is not belled, it is still a cat and to identify, characterize and count. The cats in the dark are also troublesome. It is similar to conducting a prior art search exercise At the present day, with the number of search engines and databases available for journal literatures, patents and open reports, we could search a subject matter and analyze online, but we cannot be 100 percent sure that we have captured all the references in that particular filed or subject. The search could be "comprehensive" but no one could guarantee that is "complete." By chance, if we miss a prior art reference because of the "search architecture" or the inability of "search database" to cover non-English literature, a researcher's thesis job may turn into the re-invention of a wheel. Hard-earned data over several years could turn into a futile exercise.

The question is why the researchers are reluctant for a thorough, comprehensive literature search. In those days when online literature search was limited and not so efficient for journal and patent literatures, we were used to going to the library. I can recall an entire day-long search for my research topic in the Chemical Abstract section made me seem like a tired worker in a coal mine. Year by year manual search was troublesome, time-consuming and incomplete. Shantanu was not wrong that a judgement of "novelty" by the journal examiner is a better option than to ponder the time over reading a pile of heavy volumes of chemical abstracts in the IIT library. It was not possible to cover the entire research area by a manual search, and a PhD student would have preferred to devote the time on the projects. Nowadays, researchers and PhD students have access to efficient search databases, multiple online sources for journals, patent literatures and open reports. However, I found that many of them are still reluctant to conduct a background search. What could be the reason?

Cat is nowhere?

The first reason for not doing the background literature search by research students is their ignorance about IP and over-dependence on the research guide. For many groups, the junior researchers follow the footsteps of seniors and continue the research from where a senior left his thesis. It obviously provides a cushion as the knowledge transfer includes a comprehensive background search. Many research guides are specialize in a specific topics and the groups know almost everything about competitions in their respective research areas. Each group even has selected journals where research articles are published and the continuous examination of the manuscripts is a valuable source of background search or an updated search. However, for a patent application from a research group specialized in a technical area, the researchers do not bother too much about the novelty or patentability. It is because of their limitations in IP knowledge. Only few research groups consider IP as an integral part of research.

For a researcher working a in a group of diversified portfolio has a high-risk for missing a prior art document. The researcher needs to be on his own many a times with limited knowledge on the online literature search process and IP. Sometimes, the researchers have to assume that there is no such document that exists like the process or product as he/she has invented and explained in the manuscript or in the thesis.

As the researcher's main objective is to get academic excellence and obtain a degree at the end, the application part of the applied research topic carries not much importance. If I ask a researcher about the possibility of "freedom to practice" for his invention, either the response would be diverted to his research guide or would be marked as the topic related to the legal only. Honestly, I did not hear the terms like *patentability* or *freedom to practice* during my research days. None of my research colleagues heard those for sure. I assumed my idea and process were unique. After several years, I found that no one actually asked me the questions, "What is the novelty in your research project? Is it your process that was novel, or the product? or a novel product by a process?" If I do not know what is meant by the word "novelty," how can I perform a background search? Even I had a vague idea of the difference between "discovery" and "invention." If the research project topic of a student is neither an invention nor a discovery, no one would file an infringement suit until the research outcome gets transformed into a commercial process which delivers a competitive edge.

Spot the cats

Many a times, the research topic remains as an academic interest only. If at all it is related to the applied field, neither does it remain scalable nor does it have industrial applicability. So, why should a researcher indulge in the luxury of learning IP? I can find more than one reason:

1. A comprehensive background search would augment the quality or research and thesis. A researcher could justify the "novel" process or product based on the existing related prior arts.

2. If a researcher finds that the research topic is not "novel" as revealed by a background research at an early stage of the research, he has time to "design around."

3. Understanding the "novelty" is important even if no patent application has been submitted as a part of research project. Still, it is necessary to check the "freedom to practice." This would ensure the possible "commercialization" of the process or product in the near future.

APPENDIX

Stepwise Patent Filing Process:
From the Desk of Sniffer Dog

The entire process of patent filing and getting it granted could be subdivided into five steps. These are in the form of personal recommendations in order to facilitate the patenting process.

Inception of data: Defining the invention

The first step in the generation of intellectual property is the inception of an idea to address or resolve some technical problems, or an alternative/better way to resolve a problem. At this stage, the inventor does not know if the "idea" is a novel or he/she has just reinvented the wheel. To demonstrate that the idea could work, it needs an infrastructure. However, this is a time-consuming effort. Suppose the initial "belief" is that the idea is novel, then the first step towards IP protection would be to file a "**provisional application,**" which would secure the "date of invention." The filing of the "provisional application" has a two-fold advantage. First, it would secure the inventor a "date of invention" as a filing date and, if anyone comes up with the same idea before the inventor develops/configures the invention further, the inventor still holds the "priority" to get his claim granted on the basis of the "earlier priority date." Second, the inventor gets a "lifeline" for a year from the date of filing of the "provisional" application to work on his invention, shape that better and generate more data to file a full patent application—called a "non-provisional application." The filing of the provisional application is cheap and, if further development of the invention and data collection are not accomplished within a year, the inventor could drop the idea. Then, there is no obligation to file a "non-provisional" application. Even later on, the same inventor could start working on the same invention, as a "provisional" application never gets published and it would never be shown as a prior art against his application later on. The "secret" will remain as "secret" with the patent office. Only, the inventor can't claim the priority if the full-fledged "non provisional" application is filed more than a year from the date of filing of the provisional application.

However, before a provisional application is drafted and filed online, the **IP analyst recommends a novelty search**. At this point, the claim is not drafted and no data/supportive information is available but, based on the "idea" shared, a quick novelty search could be carried out. This could help the inventor to get information about possible competition (players/competitors/technologies) in the specific technology domain. On that basis, the **IP analyst** could guide the inventors to reshape the idea, broaden the concept or limit it. So, it is not a "blind filing" of patent application in the form of a "provisional." Rather, an analyst can provide a patent strategy at the beginning of the IP generation. An IP analyst, who is also a subject-matter expert, would recommend the inclusion of possible adjacent areas in the "provisional" patent application (possible white spaces) so that the inventor does not miss out anything during the filing of the "non-provisional" application at a later stage.

The Discovery

The discovery phase, as per IP analysts, takes place after the provisional filing in many cases. Surprizing, but true. The inventor generates sufficient data to prove that the idea/technology works. At this point, the inventor must look to maximize the gains from the patenting. **An IP analyst** recommends a "**Patent and Technical Landscape**" at this step. This would be of a great help in many ways. A patent landscape could provide comprehensive information on how much of the adjacent technical areas that could be covered (white spaces available), identifying key competitors, the technology trends and possible "blockages." So, the inventor could remain prepared for possible "office actions" long before the application gets submitted. Even the inventor could include the related references (patent and non-patent literatures) later in the non-provisional application and put forward a strong justification for patentability. Patent and literature landscaping are done in a manner that they cover a broad area so that they can serve the purpose for the present application, also create a foundation for a possible next patent application in same technical areas and would help the inventor to generate the next idea. You may call it an innovative way to create an innovation.

The Development

The invention takes shape during this stage. The inventor gathers more data as well as the examples and comparative examples necessary to support the invention. The scope of the invention and how much the technical area could be claimed those could be analyzed in this step. In a nutshell, it is called the "scope of invention." Once the scope of the invention becomes clear, the patent drafter gets engaged in regular meetings with the inventor. The draft claims are construed and the claim language is checked. Based on the claims construed, the IP analyst conducts a **patentability search** to look for any related prior art (prior invention) that might be available in patent, journals, literatures or in any other public documents. Based on the patentability search report, the claims are revised if needed. The scope of the invention could be further broadened or made limited. A patentability search report is also served as a source for citing appropriate references as background for the patent application.

The Demonstration

On the basis of a patentability search report shared by the IP analyst, the patent application and claims are revised with more precision. The patent analyst looks for additional scope to cover if the opportunity is found. It involves gathering of some new data in the form of examples and comparative examples, if applicable. In this phase, the patent drafter and the analyst work hand-in-hand to make a final patent application supported by the patentability search report. It is like demonstrating the skill to successfully address a series of mock office actions. This would definitely reduces the risk against the possible resistance during real office action (by the patent office) and possible opposition/infringements against such application in the future. Once, the final draft is prepared, the patent agent initiates the process for filing a "non-provisional" application online. An IP analyst could also recommend a mock **Freedom to Practice** search prior to the patent application so that the inventor could get some short of assurance that the invention could be practicable commercially if the application is granted.

Filing a patent application through a good IP professional means it goes through a comprehensive de-risking to ensure an inventor gets the maximum benefit from the application.

The Deployment

IP analyst support does not end with filing the patent application. They treat the filing as a first step towards securing the IP. The IP analyst also provides support during the questions and objections raised by the patent office (office actions). IP analysts are subject matter experts in technical fields, duly trained in IP law and could fight to protect your claims and continuously justify them as a techno-legal support.

The patent filing process is a journey and IP analysts support inventors till the grant of the patent and beyond.

In case of an opposition or infringement by a third party, they also help with references and prosecution support.

The "sniffer dog" stays alert—before the battle, during the battle and beyond the battle.

End note

I convey my sincere thanks as you have completed reading this book as a short journey through IP strategy (patent). I assume that you have understood some part of patent strategies in the form of situation-based stories. If you have any suggestions to improve the narration or you have any question or need clarifications, please write to me at tarakranjan.gupta@yahoo.com. I am also available in LinkedIn at: https://www.linkedin.com/in/tarakranjan-gupta-a76ba513

www.ingramcontent.com/pod-product-compliance
Lightning Source LLC
Chambersburg PA
CBHW030801180526
45163CB00003B/1121

9 781637 814307